YOU WERE BORN FOR THIS

YOU WERE BORN FOR THIS

Astrology for Radical Self-Acceptance

CHANI NICHOLAS

HarperOne
An Imprint of HarperCollinsPublishers

HarperCollins books may be purchased for educational, business, or sales pro-
motional use. For information, please email the Special Markets Department at
SPsales@harpercollins.com.

FIRST HARPERCOLLINS PAPERBACK EDITION PUBLISHED IN 2021

Designed by Michelle Crowe

Illustrations by Karen McClellan

Library of Congress Cataloging-in-Publication Data is available upon request.

ISBN 978-0-06-304377-0

22 23 24 25 26 LBC 11 10 9 8 7

This book, this life, this work does not exist without my love, my best friend, my partner in all things, my wife.

Sonya Priyam Passi.

You gather me daily. You captivate me endlessly. You inspire me to discover what is possible and what is beyond that. You are the bravest, most compassionate person I have ever met. You are my Fortuna, my greatest blessing, and my calling. I thank the heavens for you every moment of every day.

Your love is the most powerful force I have ever known. It has transformed every wound into a lesson, every heartbreak into a moment that no longer owns me, every obstacle into an opportunity. It is an indomitable force that surrounds, protects, and uplifts me. Being your partner is my greatest privilege, my honor, and my most precious gift.

I know every day that I lived before meeting you was in preparation for you. Meeting you activated my potential in ways I could never have imagined. It is no mistake that when we came together everything else in my world fell into place. Thank you for finding me, keeping me, and creating this incredible life with me.

CONTENTS

III

THE FIRST KEY: YOUR SUN 37

Your Life's Purpose

YOU WERE BORN FOR THIS

INTRODUCTION

BEING WITNESSED

The first time I encountered astrology was the first time I remember feeling seen. I was eight years old. Living in a small town snuggled in the base of the Rockies, I was surrounded by both the immeasurable beauty of nature and the unforgiving wreckage of addiction. I spent a lot of my childhood alone. While the adults in my life partied and self-destructed with wanton abandon, I watched *The Cosby Show* and dreamed of a life with parents, siblings, grandparents, and a lineage to claim me. When the party came home, I felt a different kind of loneliness. An overdose, a fatal accident, a shotgun fired, a conviction. I knew what cocaine tasted like by the time I was five. I knew not to tell anyone about anything that happened in my home. I was terrified all the time. So I hid. I hid in any bathroom with a lock on the door. I hid inside a self-constructed personality that was aloof, sarcastic, and remote. I hid to protect my excruciatingly sensitive and porous being from the sharp edges of adult sorrows that swallowed my childhood.

As those around me wreaked havoc, it wasn't uncommon for me to find myself in some makeshift shack up a dirt road, with adults I did not want to be with, witnessing events that I was unable to make sense of or navigate. I was in such a situation on that fateful day I first encountered astrology. A total stranger, a skinny, white woman with unkept hair and an unloved look in her eyes, gave me a gift I have never forgotten. Armed with only my birthdate, she looked up the location of the planets on the day I was born, gazed at me with a glimmer in her eye, and said, "You're very judgmental."

Yes. Yes I am, I thought with pride.

I had no real idea what that word actually meant, but I immediately resonated with what I felt it implied. She was distinguishing me from my surroundings. She saw that I possessed the kind of discernment that others around me lacked. I had judgment, and, with it, I would find a way out of this mess.

Though I never met her again, that brief interaction gave me something to hold on to. It may have only been a thread, but when that's all you've got it feels like spun gold. In a situation that threatened to obliterate me, someone looked down at a book of symbols and numbers and used astrology to uncover a truth about me that would save my life.

Being witnessed is essential to our humanity, our growth, and our ability to move past the trauma that we have survived. If astrology does its job, it offers a mirror in which we see both our best selves and our growth edges.

RADICAL SELF-ACCEPTANCE

When I was twelve years old, I had my first thorough natal chart reading. My father had just moved across the country to Toronto with my second stepmother, a woman I had grown up with. I had spent many weekends with her and her two children. Our childhoods were parallel. Our parents had partied, worked, and teetered on the brink of madness together. We were witnesses to some of each other's most harrowing moments and we had survived. The fact that my father and their mother fled the small town we grew up in meant that they were ready to leave behind (at least some) of the violence, drugs, and self-destruction we had all been so embroiled in.

The trauma bonds between us all were solid, and for a moment, it seemed like together we might be able to heal the collective heartbreak of the past decade. We were a rag-tag bunch, shell-shocked, from a small town, a family of misfits looking for another chance at life in the Big City.

My new step-grandmother, Anita, was a reiki master. Besides being the most captivating, witchy, spiritual, tell-it-like-it-is healer woman I had ever met, she had a collection of friends who were equally talented in the healing arts and as weird as she was. Psychics, astrologers, past-life explorers, artists, and the like surrounded her, and me, when I got to spend time in Toronto. All the people that I met through her seemed to be dedicated to living less harmful lives. They spent their time developing their healing practices, and knowing them gave me a glimpse of another way of being.

Shortly after the move, Anita gifted the family with a reading from Taina Ketola, an astrologer she knew and had worked with. Taina lived in a small town just outside the city, in a normal-looking house, in a subdued, suburban subdivision. Inside, the world she constructed for me was anything but. As soon as she started describing each one of us, I was mesmerized. I was hearing this symbolic language for the first time, but I felt like I had always known it. Explaining the intricacies of our charts with great skill and humor, she helped me to understand how and why we were each coping with the situation we were in differently, and how we would each cope with life in general. The distinctions that she was able to make between us helped me understand myself in relation to everyone else, which is always useful, but in a new family unit is essential. She had written a book, *The New Astrology*, which my father bought for me. It became my bible. As a child in search of any kind of wisdom and guidance, astrology became my immediate, full-blown obsession, but it would be decades before I finally accepted it as my path.

I am a late bloomer. Like a late, late bloomer. Astrologers warned me that with a Saturn placement such as mine, it might be the case, but it's hard to understand what that might actually mean when you hear it at a young age. I had tons of drive, but the only place I knew to put it was therapy, reiki workshops with Anita, spiritual ritual, self-help books, affirmations, meditations, episodes of *Oprah*, and astrology. I spent my twenties largely in a healing incubator. To support myself I did community work, astrology readings, reiki sessions, a lot of waitressing, bartending, cleaning, temping, and whatever else would pay the bills. Though I knew giving astrology readings was a way to make money, I didn't feel emotionally, psychologically, or structurally strong enough to do so. Exclusively doing readings was also never quite enough for me. Though it is an honor to read people's charts, I've always known that I wanted a larger outlet than only one-to-one work. Before social media, however, those outlets were open to only a select few. My business as it exists today wasn't an option when I was twenty. Sometimes we are late bloomers because the world needs to catch up to us.

The truth is that I felt lost for most of my professional life. By my early thirties, I was working long hours, teaching yoga to folks from all kinds of backgrounds and situations—celebrities, cancer patients, those experiencing homelessness, and folks in systems of mass incarceration. My work was in the healing realm, but I still felt unfulfilled. I wasn't living my purpose, and it haunted me. I didn't want to be part of the Yoga Industrial Complex. I didn't want to be teaching a spiritual and physical discipline that came from a culture that wasn't my own. I didn't want to be another white lady culturally appropriating Indian spirituality. I searched and searched for something to do. I whined. I was bitter about the fact that it wasn't easy for me.

Meanwhile, I dreamt about the planets constantly. I talked about astrology in therapy, and, when I did, my therapist would say, "You know, every time you talk about astrology you light up, the energy comes into the room, your entire being shifts." And I would stare blankly at her, annoyed that she didn't understand my crisis.

I was deeply frustrated, really broke, and not getting any younger. So I did what any person in their midthirties does when they can't figure out what to do next.

I went back to school.

I finished my BA at CIIS in San Francisco, where a group of thoughtful, compassionate, and brilliant educators helped to reawaken within me my need to be involved in social justice work and my need for and love of writing. At the same time, social media was shifting our way of communicating with each other, and I was reengaging with astrology in a new way because of it.

I didn't want to be an astrologer: in my mind it wasn't a "real" profession. I wanted to be something respectable. After growing up in a town filled with so much make-believe and escapism, I wanted something that would ground me in the world and be of real, practical use to others. How could astrology give me that?

The planets had a few ideas. They were still visiting me in my dreams like they always had, only now they were getting louder and more domineering, waking me up terrified in the middle of the night. It seemed like the only way to quiet them was to oblige. Armed with a blogspot and my first awkward and jumbled horoscopes, I started writing—not because I thought anyone would like my brand of astro-political self-help (I was certain, in fact, that people would hate it), but because I felt like if I didn't channel everything that was awakening within me, it would backfire on my system.

It still took a few more years of self-doubt, failed attempts at finding a meaningful career elsewhere, and dropping out of three master's programs before I finally decided to give it my all. I had worn myself out. I had tried everything else I could think of. I kept returning to what my therapist and others had told me before. This is where the energy was. When I spoke about astrology I came to life. It was easy for me to dismiss that when I was younger, but as I aged I realized how rare it really was. When we turn toward the things that fill us with a sense of purpose, energy, and enthusiasm, we become a channel for more of the same.

Writing horoscopes gave me a connection to the outside world. I was still single, without much in the way of family, and painfully lonely most days, but writing felt like (then and now) a love affair. I was actively carving a place for myself in the world, and I could sense that it was the start of something I had been searching for my whole life. A couple of years into writing horoscopes, I started formally studying traditional astrology with Demetra George, and in doing so I came to realize that astrology, ritual, and working with people in the way I was beginning to was right there in my birth chart. Clear as day. Waiting for me to see it, accept it, and own it. Soon after, I met the woman who would become my wife, and all the pieces of my life started to fall quickly into place.

Astrology has helped me to accept my past, present, and future potential more radically and with greater certainty than anything else has. This book is offered to you in the hope that it will validate your deepest desires and dreams for your life while challenging you to accept the responsibility of bringing them into being.

I

YOUR BIRTH CHART

THE BLUEPRINT OF YOUR POTENTIAL

Your birth chart is a snapshot of the sky the moment you took your first breath. It marks your arrival here on earth; a celestial blueprint, if you will, that holds the keys to living a life of purpose. Popular astrology has focused heavily on one part of the astrological alphabet: your Sun sign. While the Sun may have been in Sagittarius when you were born, that is only one small part of what was occurring in the sky. You have every planet and every sign somewhere in your chart. Astrology represents the entirety of life and, like life, we escape none of it. You are not just a Virgo or a Gemini or a Libra; you are a moment in time, with every sign, planet, and point playing a part in who you are, how you move through the world and what you came here to do.

Whatever pattern constellated in the heavens at the moment you took your first breath is the cosmic imprint of your soul, the map of the journey you will take in this lifetime, and the ways in which you will go about it. Whether Mars marks your chart in a prominent way—stirring controversy and courageous acts from you—or Jupiter is in charge of your life's direction—encouraging you to open doors through optimism and generosity—you, like everyone and everything else here, are an amulet of celestial significance.

The positions of the planets in your birth chart reveal the nature of your life without any kind of judgment attached. Your astrological makeup is a neutral reflection of your life, much like a mirror. Only the person looking at the reflection judges it; the mirror simply reveals what is there. Astrology reminds us that we are exactly as we are supposed to be for good reason. On purpose and with a purpose that we must live out if we want to feel any kind of fulfillment.

THE THREE KEYS OF YOUR CHART

There are three keys in every chart that fundamentally explain your life's purpose, your physical and emotional needs, and your motivation for living. It is almost embarrassing to admit that the meaning of my chart was not crystal clear to me until my late thirties. I had pored over it for decades. I had gotten lost down a million rabbit holes trying to understand its most obscure angles. I had received many readings, by many talented astrologers, but until I had the tools of traditional astrology in my grasp and could understand my chart through these three simple keys, I could not see the blueprint of my life that they represented. The specifics of my potential were just vague references to a future that felt like it was constantly eluding me. That is why I am so passionate about teaching you how to understand your chart in this way.

The three keys are

1. ☉ **Sun**—your life's purpose

2. ☾ **Moon**—your physical and emotional needs

3. ⛎ **Ascendant and Its Ruler**—your motivation for living and the direction your life is steered in

By the end of this book, you'll understand each of these three keys in your chart and have the tools for unlocking them. They will anchor your understanding of yourself, your life, and its meaning, and aid in your ability to love and accept yourself as you are. Understanding our astrology chart is the doorway; the effort to move through it is our own.

The Sun in your chart will detail the nature of how and where you need to shine. The Moon in your chart will tell you how you can best unpack your life's purpose daily, with great care and consideration for your unique physical and emotional needs. The sign of your Ascendant will detail the specific kind of motivation that you have for living your life. The planet that rules your Ascendant will tell you the direction that your life is steered in.

Everything else in your chart will either be supporting or challenging these keys or, for our purposes here, they will be secondary.

PULLING UP YOUR CHART

Download the CHANI app to pull up your birth chart on your phone, or go to my site at www.ChaniNicholas.com. You will need your day, month, year, location, and time of birth to pull up an accurate birth chart. Time is everything in astrology. The more accurate your birth time, the more accurate your birth chart. Spending extra effort investigating the exact time of your birth is always worthwhile.

WHAT IF YOU DON'T KNOW YOUR BIRTH TIME?

If you don't know your birth time offhand, is it on your birth certificate? If not, I recommend ordering a long-form birth certificate, specifically requesting that it have your birth time on it. You can also contact the hospital where you were born to obtain your birth records. Failing that, do you have any living relative or family friend who might remember or a baby book that includes it?

If not, there are a couple of options available to you. The first is rectification, which is the process of trying to figure out your time of birth by using whatever data you have and the timing of life events that you are sure about. It is a little lengthy and costly, and it can never guarantee your birth time, but many are very happy with the results. Find an astrologer who does this work and who can help you figure out your approximate birth time by working with the most important life events that you can recall.

The other option is to work with what you have, knowing you'll be engaging with astrology but in a much less specific way. You won't know what houses your planets or signs are in, but you will still derive a lot of information about the strengths and challenges of your astrological makeup by being able to see what signs your planets are in and what relationships the planets are making to each other in your chart. You won't know what your Ascendant is, or what the ruler of the Ascendant is, which is one of the keys outlined in this book. However, knowing about your Sun and Moon, and their relationships to the other planets in your chart, can still offer a lot of valuable astrological data to work with. The pattern in the sky will still reveal something specific and informative about your life's calling.

It's important to get to know your chart in its entirety, not just a list of the signs that the planets were in when you were born. That list is helpful, but there is something that awakens within us when we see the diagram of the sky the moment we took our first breath. Being able to locate the planets in the houses and seeing the connections they are making to one another is how we learn astrology.

Once you take a look at your chart, you might find yourself overwhelmed by all the patterns in it. Each new piece of information can take time to integrate. Embrace this for what it is: a journey, not something to be mastered or done with precision on your first go. Though some realizations do come quickly, others will be missed for long periods of time.

This process takes patience, compassion, and humility. Many of us come to astrology in search of ourselves. In search of the meaning of our lives. In search of some clues about what it is we are here to do and whether or not we are on the right track. Your astrological chart will show you all that and more if you have the patience to learn its language and wade through its sometimes slow ways of revealing answers to you.

Demetra George has said that, like other wisdom traditions, astrology is a self-secret system, meaning that until the student is ready to learn, the teachings aren't totally accessible. Until we are open to understanding something about ourselves and our chart, it will evade us. Astrology, like any healing practice, works best with time and layering of information. Astrology is a symbolic language that speaks to both our logical brain and our unconscious mind. Once you are ready, it will flood you with its insights, illuminating the archetypes that you are living out, the lessons that they are teaching you, and the ways in which you can channel the energy in your life. It can take years sometimes to get the insights that we need, but they always come at exactly the right time.

Even when we understand the words spoken to us, it can be hard to comprehend what they might mean for us in the moment. Understanding our astrological chart requires us to understand ourselves, which takes work. We need to develop a willingness to be introspective, contemplative, reflective, and curious about how we move through the world and how the world may respond.

Hold the tools of astrology with an unrelenting respect for their power and with the awareness that it takes a long time to understand what they are communicating and what they are capable of.

COMMITTING TO THIS PROCESS

I remember one astrologer telling me that, upon looking at my chart, they had no idea how I'd ever let myself be loved. I understood what they meant because I knew what they were looking at in my chart, but I felt completely pathologized by their take on my ability to overcome the challenges my chart presented. In that moment, I struggled not to give that astrologer, someone I had looked up to for years and still do, power over my life and its path. It took me a minute, but in the end I chose to believe that I was capable of healing. I was not beyond repair. I found love. I discovered that I am actually very attuned to giving and receiving it, in conditions where I can thrive.

Our preconceived notion of ourselves, or others' notions of us, can dominate our worldview and make us miss the point of our lives and our astrology entirely.

Consider making the following agreements with yourself, with me as your guide for the moment, and with the system of astrology in general, before going any farther in this book or aspect of your study:

1. **I promise to never give my current understanding of my chart too much power.**

It is a guarantee that while learning about your astrological makeup, you will misunderstand what you are looking at. Most likely for a good long while.

We humans are, unfortunately, incredibly fearful beings. We tend to project our worries and biases onto everything that we encounter, even more so when we are trying to find an accurate reflection of ourselves. I cannot count the number of times someone has come to me panic-stricken and feeling doomed because of something that they falsely gave meaning to in their chart. When we give our chart, or anything or anyone in our life, too much power, we lose contact with our agency. Try to come at your chart with an investigative and optimistic autonomy.

2. **I promise to never underestimate the wisdom that is woven into my chart.**

As you come to understand yourself and your life in greater depth, you will also understand your chart in greater depth. Be careful not to jump to conclusions about what your chart means before you get the chance to experience, shape, and rise to the possibilities of it.

As we grow and change, so does our ability to work with the difficult aspects of our lives. With time and effort, we are able to more deftly and intelligently engage with what pains us. You will come to appreciate the harder aspects of your chart and your life if you are committed to your own healing. What appears appalling at first can become a gold mine of possibilities if we come prepared to be transformed by it.

3. **I promise to always leave room for learning, unlearning, and re-learning.**

No matter what you learn about your chart, you have the power to grow, heal, change, and evolve. No astrological signature can take that power from you. Whether our charts are easy or challenging, we are all charged with the task of becoming. Only you can choose your own growth.

HOW TO USE THIS BOOK

As you start to delve into this material, it's always good to sit with each piece that you learn. Write things down that are particularly resonant. Take breaks from the material. Let what strikes you as true sink in. Dream about it. Bring it to therapy, your trusted friends, and mentors.

The framework of this book is both a guide and a workbook. At the end of each big piece of learning that you'll do, there will be reflection questions that you can participate in to the level that you wish to. I will do my best to guide you through this journey of self-discovery as we cover basic definitions and begin to develop a deeper understanding of all that your chart is communicating to you.

Treat this book as a choose-your-own-adventure sort of experience. We'll explore your Sun, Moon, Ascendant, and its ruler in great detail. Skip ahead to the section that explains your particular setup. Make notes. Work with the reflection questions and affirmations that are helpful to you. Come and go as you feel ready to absorb new information about your chart. You can also use this book to work through someone else's chart if they have given you permission to do so. This is your journey. Your adventure. I am just one of many guides along the way.

Throughout this book, I refer to the charts of Dr. Maya Angelou and Frida Kahlo, two people who left behind rich autobiographical legacies that helped shape culture, art, and their respective professions. I chose them not only because their work has been deeply meaningful to so many, myself included, but also because, on a more practical level, we have verified birth times for them—not something that is always easy to come by. In addition, they have both fully lived out their lives and left this earth, so we do not have to guess at any unlived future potential.

READING CHECKLIST

Before you go farther, gather the following items:

- *Your chart*

- *Pen, paper, highlighters*

- *Your journal*

- *Water and snacks*

Creating an Altar in Honor of Your Chart

Altars are spaces that we intentionally create to mark moments that are important to us. Altars don't need to be religious or spiritual in any way if that isn't a framework that resonates with you. They are spaces where we do psychological and emotional healing, and should be specific to your needs, style, culture, and level of commitment.

If you like, you can build an altar for the work that we do together in this book as a way of holding your experience and marking this journey. Add to your altar as you learn about your astrological chart to bring it to life and into physical existence. As you read about each planet, consider going to my website to learn more about their properties and the colors, tastes, smells, herbs, foods, metals, and minerals that they rule to gain a deeper insight into their nature and the different ways in which they may be manifesting for you.

When building an altar, start with a clean and clear space, preferably in the east. Altars are best created in a neutral environment. If you have a table, counter, or shelf that you can dedicate to an altar, it's good to keep it in the same place so that you somatically know that being in that space means you are doing some kind of healing work.

Your altar can be as simple or elaborate as you like. A candle, a flower, and an intention are enough to begin with. As you learn about your Sun, Moon, and ruler of your Ascendant, feel free to place things on your altar that represent them and any planet in relationship to them, as a way of honoring and getting to know them better.

II

THE BASICS

Let's start with the basics—in your chart, there are planets, signs, houses, and aspects. Understanding what they are and how they play together is essential.

THE WHO: PLANETS

In astrology the planets are described as the "who" of our charts. They are the different characters in the play of our lives. Some seem like they are out to get us, foiling our every plot, while others are always supporting our storyline. For example, Saturn and Mars are generally going to test us (or others) before they grant us their gifts. On the other hand, Jupiter and Venus may give us love and luck up front without asking for much in return. Each planet, like each character in a play, is necessary. Too much of anyone is overwhelming, and we need everyone to tell the full story. Planets have specific qualities that create conditions in our bodies, lives, and relationships.

The traditional planets and their roles are

☿ **Mercury**—The Messenger

♀ **Venus**—The Lover

♂ **Mars**—The Warrior

♃ **Jupiter**—The Sage

♄ **Saturn**—The Taskmaster

The modern planets and their roles are

♅ **Uranus**—The Revolutionary

♆ **Neptune**—The Dreamer

♇ **Pluto**—The Transformer

THE HOW: SIGNS

Each sign has its own way of functioning, its own flair, its own signature style. Each planet in your chart has to function in the style of the sign it is in. For example, Mars, planet of courage, drive, and desire, when in Aries is action-oriented and extra fast.

In Virgo, it's aggressively thorough. In Pisces, it's a seeker of great escapes and spiritual sustenance. Mars has a job to do, but how it does it varies by sign.

The signs and their styles are

♈ **Aries**—independent, action-oriented

♉ **Taurus**—stabilizing, grounded

♊ **Gemini**—communicative, curious

♋ **Cancer**—sensitive, caring

♌ **Leo**—self-expressive, creative

♍ **Virgo**—discerning, thoughtful

♎ **Libra**—social, likable

♏ **Scorpio**—intense, penetrating

♐ **Sagittarius**—adventurous, positive

♑ **Capricorn**—enduring, reserved

♒ **Aquarius**—intellectual, insightful

♓ **Pisces**—intuitive, creative

Modalities and Elements

Each sign is categorized by modality and element. There are three modalities (cardinal, fixed, and mutable) and four elements (fire, earth, air, and water).

MODALITIES

The modality of a sign tells us what its job is. Cardinal signs initiate new seasons. Fixed signs stabilize the existing season. Mutable signs let go of one season in preparation for another. Because of this, no two fire, earth, air, or water signs work exactly alike.

THE CARDINAL SIGNS

♈ **Aries** initiates action

♋ **Cancer** initiates emotional ties, bonds and feelings

♎ **Libra** initiates relationships

♑ **Capricorn** initiates the long-term plan

THE FIXED SIGNS

♉ **Taurus** harnesses the power of the material world

♌ **Leo** harnesses the power of the persona

♏ **Scorpio** harnesses the power of its emotional intensity

♒ **Aquarius** harnesses the power of its intellect

THE MUTABLE SIGNS

♊ **Gemini** disperses information

♍ **Virgo** disperses skills

♐ **Sagittarius** disperses enthusiasm

♓ **Pisces** disperses dreams and visions

ELEMENTS

There are four elements: fire, earth, air, and water. Each element has its own temperament. The element of a sign will tell you whether it functions via inspiration, practicality, communication, or emotion.

FIRE

Qualities: Spontaneous. Enthusiastic. Inspired. Self-Expressive. Intuitive.

♈ **Aries** takes initiative (cardinal) that demonstrates its personal courage and ability to act on its own inspiration (fire).

♌ **Leo** stabilizes (fixed) a warm and entertaining persona in hopes of gaining attention and having its creative self-expression (fire) witnessed.

♐ **Sagittarius** seeks unrestricted movement (mutable), and freedom, to find meaning that illuminates (fire) its purpose in a buoyant and positive manner.

EARTH

Qualities: Grounding. Stabilizing. Manifesting. Generative. Hardworking.

♉ **Taurus** develops security through stabilizing (fixed) its resources and developing them into fertile (earth) fields from which it can provide much abundance.

♍ **Virgo** wants a diversity (mutable) of skills (earth) to serve life with. Through perfecting its craft, Virgo creates meaning for itself.

♑ **Capricorn** initiates (cardinal) disciplined action in order to accomplish great feats. Through its ability to utilize the tools (earth) it has access to, Capricorn develops the self-restraint necessary to climb any mountain.

AIR

Qualities: Intellectual. Focused on ideas and facts. Strong communicator.

♊ **Gemini** disperses (mutable) information (air), connecting to many through intellectually stimulating exchanges that generate new ideas and relationships.

♎ **Libra** initiates (cardinal) relationships (air), seeking balance, harmony, and justice.

♒ **Aquarius** articulates (air) its well-developed ideas in a self-assured (fixed) way.

WATER

Qualities: Intuitive. Emotive. Impressionistic. Sensitive. Responsive.

69 **Cancer** initiates (cardinal) familial bonds through demonstrating care (water).

♏ **Scorpio** penetrates (fixed) the secret and mysterious (water) aspects of life.

♓ **Pisces** connects to a vast array of experiences through being open and impressionable (mutable) to its surroundings and offering compassion (water) to many.

Homes, Thrones, and Hostile Environments

Each traditional planet has two signs in which it feels at home, two signs in which it feels uncomfortable, one sign in which it gains recognition, and one sign in which it feels disrespected.* In all other signs, it is in neutral territory.

- **Domicile**—Sign where a planet feels at home—here it has access to all its resources, can fire on all cylinders, and is as comfortable as it can be.

- **Detriment**—Sign where a planet feels uncomfortable—here it will have to work twice as hard to do its job, pushing us to stretch and grow in ways we wouldn't otherwise.

---

*Note that the Sun and Moon (collectively known as the luminaries) each have only one sign in which they feel at home, one sign in which they feel uncomfortable, one sign in which they gain notoriety, and one sign in which they feel disrespected.

- **Exaltation**—Sign where a planet gains recognition—here it will offer us gifts and blessings with little effort.

- **Fall**—Sign where a planet feels disrespected—here it will struggle to get on a level playing field, but in that struggle will help us to honor the experience of the outcast.

PLANET	DOMICILE	DETRIMENT	EXALTATION	FALL
☉ SUN	Leo	Aquarius	Aries	Libra
☽ MOON	Cancer	Capricorn	Taurus	Scorpio
☿ MERCURY	Gemini Virgo	Sagittarius Pisces	Virgo	Pisces
♀ VENUS	Taurus Libra	Aries Scorpio	Pisces	Virgo
♂ MARS	Aries Scorpio	Taurus Libra	Capricorn	Cancer
♃ JUPITER	Sagittarius Pisces	Gemini Virgo	Cancer	Capricorn
♄ SATURN	Capricorn Aquarius	Cancer Leo	Libra	Aries

THE WHERE: HOUSES

Houses are the places in our chart where the planets are located. If the planets are the actors and the signs are their styles or costumes, then the houses are the sets where their stories are lived out. Each house is a section of the sky as we see it from earth and represents a specific area of our lives. From our mental health to our money, our birth chart covers our entire existence.

The 12 houses are

- **1st House**—self, body, appearance, and vitality

- **2nd House**—assets, resources, and livelihood

- **3rd House**—communication, daily life, siblings, and extended family

- **4th House**—parents, home, and foundations

- **5th House**—children, creative projects, sex, and pleasure

- **6th House**—work and health

- **7th House**—committed partnerships

- **8th House**—death, mental health, and other people's resources

- **9th House**—travel, education, publishing, religion, astrology, and philosophy

- **10th House**—career and public roles

- **11th House**—friends, community, patrons, and good fortune

- **12th House**—hidden life, secrets, sorrow, and loss

A NOTE ON HOUSE SYSTEMS

The twelve houses in our chart represent sections of the sky. However, there is no empirical, "right" way to divide the sky. As a result, there are many different house systems that astrologers have worked with for thousands of years. I use **whole sign houses** *because it is the system that makes the most philosophical sense to me and the system that gives me the best results. Whole sign houses see each sign of the zodiac as their own place, their own house. Even if you learned about your chart using a different house system than this, the framework of whole sign houses is still a useful way of looking at your chart. Just as there are many ways to look at our life, there are many ways to look at the sky and many ways to look at the houses of our chart. Each one shifts the planets a little or a lot this way and that. Use the house system that makes the most sense to you after learning something about their logic and philosophy. In the end, it's your chart, and your understanding of it is what matters.*

The houses of our chart give us the context for where things will occur. If the Sun, for example, is in your 10th House of career, you will need to express yourself (the Sun) through professional avenues or the social roles that you hold (the 10th House). If Venus is in your 11th House of community, then much of your good fortune (11th House) comes through your ability to build relationships (Venus) with others.

Any house with a planet in it will be an important realm of life to understand, but whichever houses your Sun, Moon, and ruler of your Ascendant occupy become critical areas of life to live out, experience, and develop a relationship with. This is because those planets take special precedence as markers of life and life purpose. The more we develop a relationship to them, and the houses of our chart that they reside in, the more easily we come to understand and radically accept ourselves.

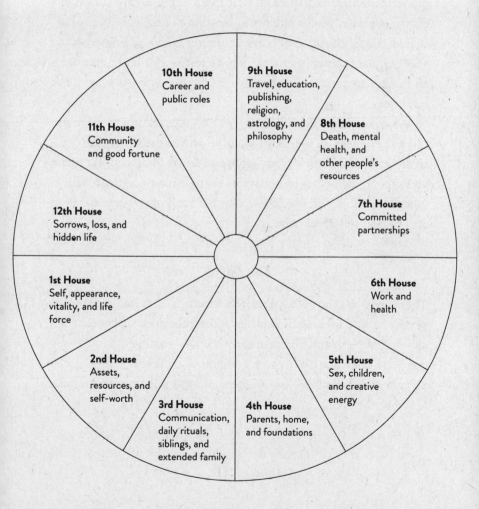

10th House Career and public roles

9th House Travel, education, publishing, religion, astrology, and philosophy

8th House Death, mental health, and other people's resources

11th House Community and good fortune

7th House Committed partnerships

12th House Sorrows, loss, and hidden life

1st House Self, appearance, vitality, and life force

6th House Work and health

2nd House Assets, resources, and self-worth

5th House Sex, children, and creative energy

3rd House Communication, daily rituals, siblings, and extended family

4th House Parents, home, and foundations

RELATIONSHIPS: ASPECTS

Aspects are the relationships that two or more planets or points have with one another. Just like all relationships, some are easy and uplifting, while others are difficult and even discouraging. We can place aspects into three categories: gifts, challenges, and mergers.

For example, if Mars is making a challenging aspect to another planet in your chart, then it will most likely create conditions that feel excessively hot, causing irritation, anger, or outbursts, as heat is a signification of Mars. If Jupiter is in a gifting aspect to another planet in your chart, then it creates a situation that feels abundant, fortunate, and positive, as Jupiter is known for these qualities.

When we make the link between the aspects in our chart and our experiences in life, both positive and negative, we can cultivate compassion for our struggle and learn to disrupt the more self-sabotaging beliefs or behaviors that we have acquired. This is where the rubber of astrology meets the road of self-actualization and radical self-acceptance.

The Gifts

There are two kinds of aspects (relationships) that fall under gifts: sextiles and trines. Both sextiles and trines are aspects that bestow gifts, blessings, and protections upon whatever planets they connect. They act like a fairy godmother or favorite auntie who always gives you love, encouragement, and a little cash on your way out the door.

- **Sextile**—planets that are two signs away from each other, one in an earth sign and one in a water sign, or one in an air sign and one in a fire sign (*signs that are 60 degrees apart from each other*).

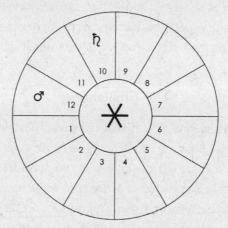

Planets in houses at a 60-degree angle from each other are sextile.

- **Trine**—planets that are four signs away from each other and in the same element as each other, e.g., two or more planets in different fire signs (*signs that are 120 degrees apart*).

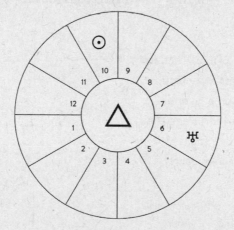

Planets in houses at a 120-degree angle from each other are trine.

Sextiles are subtler than trines, but both are positive and can be leaned on in times of turbulence and difficulty, like calling a friend when you are in a jam, need advice, or feel a little lost. A sextile from Venus is the strongest sextile that can be made (the sextile is Venus's signature aspect), and a trine from Jupiter is the strongest trine that can be made (the trine is Jupiter's signature aspect).

The Challenges

There are two kinds of aspects that fall under challenges: squares and oppositions. Both are challenging in their own way and require us to make extra effort. Squares are points of friction that encourage us to take some kind of action, but sometimes that friction only feels like a harmful abrasion. Oppositions act like tugs-of-war in which we are asked to balance opposites, integrate polarity, and come to some deeper understanding of what we project onto the world and what we must be able to reclaim for ourselves.

There are exceptions to these rules, however. Squares and oppositions from Venus and Jupiter aren't "bad," as those planets can't do harm, but they may exacerbate something specific to their nature.

- **Square**—planets that are three signs away from each other, e.g., one planet in Taurus and the other in Leo (*signs that are 90 degrees apart*).

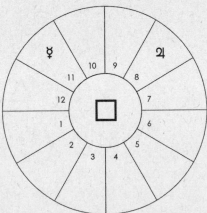

Planets in houses at a 90-degree angle from each other are square.

- **Opposition**—planets that are six signs away from each other (in opposite signs to each other), e.g., one planet in Sagittarius and the other in Gemini *(180 degrees apart).*

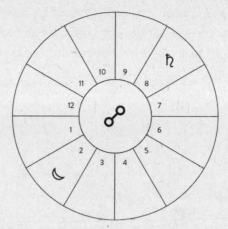

Planets in houses at a 180-degree angle from each other are in opposition.

A square from Mars is considered the most difficult square to have (the square is Mars's aspect), and an opposition from Saturn is considered the most challenging opposition to have (the opposition is Saturn's aspect). Remember that while challenging squares and oppositions create obstacles, our ability to overcome them helps us grow and move toward our purpose. Without the challenge, we might never need to put our talents to use.

The Mergers

Conjunctions (mergers) occur when any planet is in the same sign as another planet. Conjunctions are a merging or blending of energies. The closer in degree they are to each other, the greater the impact. Conjunctions with Venus and Jupiter will be helpful for connecting to others with ease (Venus) and attracting abundance (Jupiter) into our lives. Conjunctions with Mars and Saturn will be challenging, demanding that we develop the rigorous discipline (Saturn) needed to accomplish our goals or find ways in which to channel our anger into appropriate and beneficial action (Mars). Conjunctions to and from all other planets need to be considered on an individual basis (which we will do in the later chapters of this book).

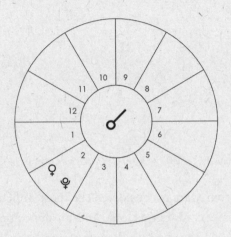

Planets in the same house are conjunct.

PUTTING IT ALL TOGETHER: THE RULES

Until they become second nature, it's helpful to keep reiterating the rules to ourselves. Archetypal languages like astrology easily become a mishmash of correlations that blur the meaning of what we are looking at. As a reminder:

- Planets are the characters in our chart.

- Signs denote the style and flair of the planets in our chart.

- Houses tell you where the planets are living out their drama and telling their stories.

- Aspects tell you which planets are challenging you, which are gifting you, and which are acting as a unit (harmoniously or not).

- Each planet is in a sign and house.

- Everyone has every planet, sign, and house in their chart. However, you may not have every type of aspect in your chart, and some of your planets might not be in relationship with any other planet in your chart.

III

THE FIRST KEY
YOUR SUN

Your Life's Purpose

Each morning the Sun rises triumphant over the eastern horizon. Reborn from a long night traveling the underworld, the Sun's rise calls us to mirror its movements. Give our gratitude. Perform our rituals. Offer ourselves up to be of service. Human life begins in the darkness of the womb, but it depends on a reliable source of light and warmth once it leaves its place of conception and incubation. The Sun in your chart is your life force. This is why it represents your life's purpose and perhaps why popular astrology has put such emphasis on the sign it is in.

Astrology is a wisdom tradition built on observation of the natural world, and we can see how the elements of the natural world have correlations with the planets in our chart. The Sun's warmth and light are what all life depends on to grow. It shines, is bright, and is luminous. All things that have those elements will be related to the Sun. Gold is its metal and color. The heart, the center of our physical system, is the organ it rules. As we notice what else in nature flourishes in the Sun, or acts like the Sun, we begin to form a deeper relationship with this system of knowledge. Astrology isn't out there, it's all around us, right here.

When the Sun is well placed in our chart, it brings with it a boundless, generative, generous, courageous, magnanimous, and glorious self-confidence. When the Sun is not well placed, it struggles to manifest itself. Much like a stormy day, the clouds and upsets of our astrological makeup can obscure the light and warmth of our soul's purpose.

For me, having a difficult aspect between my Sun and Saturn has meant that depression often wins when I am left to my own devices. Without consciously working against this aspect, I tend to settle quite easily into despair and frustration. My wife, on the other hand, who has no difficult aspects between the traditional planets that cause harm (Saturn and Mars) and her Sun, and has a very helpful one from Jupiter, planet of optimism, is and has always been prone to finding solutions and staying proactive and positive in the process. I am forever grateful for the support her chart and her heart lend to our lives and highly recommend finding those who balance you out emotionally, psychologically, and astrologically.

There are three main characteristics of your Sun that you should consider as you unpack your life's purpose:

1. The sign that it is in (how you shine)

2. The house that it is in (the area of life in which you need to shine)

3. The planets in aspect to your Sun (who is influencing your ability to shine)

CHECK IN WITH YOUR CHART

FINDING YOUR SUN

Look for this glyph ⊙ *in your chart.*
This is your Sun.

What sign is your Sun in?

My Sun is in the sign of _____.

What house is your Sun in?

My Sun is in the _____ **house of** _____.

ASPECTS TO YOUR SUN

When you pull up your chart through the CHANI app or at
www.ChaniNicholas.com, you will see which planets are in aspect
to your Sun. Remember, you may not have any planets talking to
your Sun. Don't worry about what the different aspects mean for
now. Just note them, and we will dive into their meaning soon. Fill
in the blanks below that are applicable to you.

The planets in the same sign as my Sun are _____.

The planets that are trining my Sun (four signs / 120 degrees apart)
are _____.

The planets that are sextiling my Sun (two signs / 60 degrees apart)
are _____.

The planets that are squaring my Sun (three signs / 90 degrees apart)
are _____.

The planets that are in the opposite sign from my Sun are

_____.

Key Points to Remember about Your Sun

- Your Sun is your life force, your identity, and your life's purpose.

- The sign that it is in speaks to the style in which you shine.

- The house that it is in tells you where in your life you will do this.

- Planets in aspect to your Sun either support or challenge the way in which you shine and live out your life's purpose.

SIGN OF YOUR SUN
HOW DO YOU SHINE?

What Sign Is Your Sun In?

The Sun's sign signifies the style in which we live out our life's purpose. Since the Sun is our essential self, the sign that it is in tells us about the ways in which we are comfortable shining. Not every sign likes attention, praise, or applause for the sheer sake of it. This gives some Sun signs a contradiction to work within as the Sun, left to its own devices, is a shameless and charismatic attention seeker. For example, if your Sun is in Aquarius, it is going to shine by offering the group a logical, well-thought-out system, structure, or way of understanding the world. In Libra, the Sun will shine through its ability to be in relationship with others, while in Leo, the Sun is focused on shining as brightly as possible for the sole purpose of sharing its brilliance with the world.

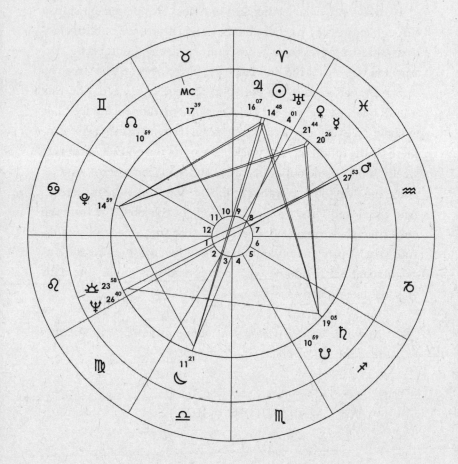

DR. MAYA ANGELOU'S BIRTH CHART

Birth Date and Time: April 4, 1928, at 2:10 p.m.

Location: St. Louis, Missouri, USA

Dr. Maya Angelou had her Sun in Aries. This placement shines through expressing its individuality and thrives when taking actions that transgress the limits culture deems appropriate. Dr. Angelou was one of the first black people to ever drive a streetcar in San Francisco, and she did so at the age of sixteen. She was initially denied the job, but Dr. Angelou's mother encouraged her to show up every day and demand that they consider her. "I sat there (at the office) for two weeks, every day. And then after two weeks, a man came out of his office and said 'come here.' And he asked me 'why do you want the job?' I said 'I like the uniforms.' And I said 'and I like people.' And so I got the job.'"* Far from the only time she would defy the limits that the American, white-supremacist patriarchy would have had her live within, Dr. Angelou spent her life doing what others said was impossible. This was just one of many firsts.

 Now it is time to choose your own adventure. Skip ahead to read the section about your Sun sign.

SUN IN ARIES

♈ ☉

The Sun in the cardinal fire sign of Aries is "exalted." Strong. Energized. Independent. In the Northern Hemisphere, the Sun's entrance into Aries is also the vernal equinox, the start of spring. From this moment on, the Sun's warmth and light grow in intensity. That intensity is carried forth in those with Sun in Aries.

The Sun "exalted" means that the Sun functions with confi-

---

*"Maya Angelou Was San Francisco's First Black Streetcar Conductor," WYNC, May 28, 2014.

dence in Aries. If your Sun is exalted, it doesn't guarantee you a life of ease and fame, but it does speak to a reservoir of strength for you to draw on when in need.

Ruled by Mars, Aries is a sign that wants to demonstrate its ability to battle. If your Sun is in Aries, you must confront the stuff of life that is most important to you, head on. As a cardinal fire sign, Aries initiates, takes action, and brings heat to any planet that resides within its domain.

Aries's symbol is the ram. Rams represent renewal, in part because when their fleece is shorn, it grows back. This gives Aries an unstoppable kind of feel. Up against any obstacle, Aries doesn't back down. It needs a little stress to make things interesting.

If you have the Sun in Aries, you are more than likely driven to prove yourself through acts of courage, bravery, and decisiveness. But that drive can easily become self-serving when the emphasis is on proving yourself right. Not every interaction is a duel, but to your Sun in Aries the conflict is sometimes too tempting to ignore. When distorted, your Sun in Aries tends toward a pushy, forceful, aggressive, arrogant, and inflammatory persona. If you have this placement, you can always benefit from the kind of self-reflection that makes a thoughtful response possible.

👁 Affirmations

- I honor my energy and its power by working at what makes me feel free.

- I am not in this alone. I remember to connect with my friends, teachers, elders, support systems, and an energy greater than myself when I need help.

📝 *Reflection Questions*

- What are you doing when you feel most energized?

- What are the battles that are important for you to engage in?

- How do you see your ability to courageously interact with the world as tied to your life's purpose? Remember that you don't have to understand exactly how this is occurring in your life at this moment, but is there a consistent desire in you to do so?

SUN IN TAURUS

The Sun in the fixed earth sign of Taurus shines when it stabilizes, steadies, and builds with the resources that it has. Taurus takes the rushing, exuberant, and unrefined energy of life and makes use of it. Molds it into a masterpiece. Cultivates the fields of its potential with its uncanny ability to manifest.

Taurus's magic might be slow, but it is also stubbornly strong. Taurus cannot be pushed, forced, or hurried. Nature doesn't rush, and neither does this bull.

The horns of the bull, the symbol for Taurus, represent fertility. In part due to the bull's domestication and use for agriculture, the horns of this magnificent beast have often been associated with the crescent Moon, the symbol of Goddess, creatrix, and giver of life. Generally, horns have been associated with the fallopian tubes, but beyond anatomy, Taurus energy is generative. Ruled by Venus, the Goddess of love and connection, Taurus has a natural fecundity.

As a fixed earth sign, Taurus is the hub. Gathering all those in need around it, if you have the Sun in Taurus, you'll most likely be energized by being generous, resourceful, and relaxed.

No one knows how to chill like a bull.

Appreciative of all things tasty, comfortable, luxurious, and sensually pleasing, your Sun in Taurus knows how to enjoy the physical realm. Your Sun in Taurus is here to build and fully enjoy a life of pleasure and productivity.

When distorted, this energy can become controlling, possessive, stubborn, and overly fixated on stability. Your Sun in Taurus may use certainty as a defense mechanism and tend toward inflexibility, bossiness, and belligerence. Because your Sun's mission is to stabilize, taking risks, changing course, or leaving halfway through a bad movie can feel like too much of a deviation from your generally consistent rhythm. You may, therefore, get stuck in your ways, ruts, and ideas about life. Your Sun in Taurus will be challenged to learn how to balance your desire for consistency with the need to take the necessary risks to support your personal growth.

👁 Affirmations

- I am allowed to change my mind.

- I am just as worthy of love and support as those to whom I offer it.

📝 Reflection Questions

- In what part of your life do you feel you are good at building, stabilizing, and creating?

- In what part of your life do you tend to get inflexible?

- How do you see your ability to build something solid or monumental as tied to your life's purpose? If you don't feel you've developed the ability to do so yet, does it sound like something that would give you satisfaction and joy?

SUN IN GEMINI
♊ ☉

In this mutable air sign that disperses information and disseminates its knowledge by way of intellectual exchange, the Sun in Gemini is never lacking something of note to contribute.

Mutable signs are naturally diverse in their interests, and Gemini, an air sign ruled by Mercury the Messenger, is intellectually so. Inquisitive to no end, your Sun in Gemini is most likely constantly searching for interesting topics of conversation to pontificate on. Contradictions, duality, and paradoxes are natural states of being for your Sun in Gemini. You need to see all sides of a theory, situation, or fact. Not exactly loyal to any one idea, Gemini roams around as many thoughts as it possibly can to get a better grasp of a subject.

The symbol for Gemini is the twins, highlighting the sign's dual nature and need for change. Like winds blowing in different directions, you can appear to be everywhere and nowhere at once. Your Sun will always need to move in ways that appear to defy the laws of gravity, time, and space. Inward and outward, reflective and responsive, introverted and extroverted, Gemini contains contradictions.

Just as its ruler, Mercury, is associated with the archetype of the magician, Gemini is a sign that appears in many different forms. If you are skilled at showing your social self, your inner twin might be revealed only to those whom you truly trust, and vice versa. Having the Sun in Gemini can mean that you become so adept at shape-shifting, you lose touch with who you are at your core.

When distorted, your Sun in Gemini can become inconsistent, distracted, gossipy, and glib. Air signs left unchecked will circulate rumors at a rate unparalleled by any other. Gemini needs to always balance its desire for a constant flow of information with discretion and integrity. When you feel too far from your base, you may need time to ground, center, and situate yourself in relationships with others who aren't charmed, fooled, or overly fascinated by your ability to weave a fantastic tale.

👁 *Affirmations*

- I don't have, nor do I need, all the answers to get where I am going.

- I trust that the information I need will reach me when I need it.

📝 *Reflection Questions*

- What kind of information do you find great joy in sharing?

- Where in your life are you a teacher? Where in your life are you a student?

- Where in your life does exchanging ideas feel like a part of your life's purpose?

SUN IN CANCER

In this cardinal water sign that initiates us into the feeling realm, the Sun is an unassumingly potent emotional force. True to its mascot, the crab, Cancer scuttles sideways, away from confrontation. Moody as the tides it rides, however, a crab backed into a corner will come out snapping, and hold on to whatever it can.

Your Sun in Cancer holds all memory. Cancer is the primordial waters of creation, the womb of humanity that carries with it our entire human story and every feeling we've had about it. If you have the Sun in Cancer, your waters run deep. Cancer is known to be the most caring, nurturing sign of the zodiac. When you love someone, they'll know it.

Your Sun shines when forming emotional bonds with others. Water signs are reflective. Ruled by the Moon, Cancer's job is to mirror the light of others. Like a parent or caregiver, you are always sensing what others need to hear, know, or receive as support. Your Sun in Cancer wants to create spaces where bonding can occur. Unafraid of intense emotional experiences, your Sun in this water sign may need you to purify yourself from the impact of the emotional residue you unassumingly soak up. Old resentments poison your waters. A regular therapeutic flushing out of the psychological system helps you feel more vital and alive.

Your Sun in Cancer is exceptionally good at intuiting and meeting the needs of others. A natural caretaker, your Sun in Cancer might hold on to an emotional slight, but it will also remember your loved ones' favorite restaurant, movie, or teacher from high school.

Cancer is as changeable as the Moon that rules it. When distorted, your Sun in Cancer can become a personality that is known for its moody, melancholy ways. Morbidly defensive and attached to the past, your Sun in Cancer can easily swing between martyrdom and irritability when too much care goes out and not enough comes in.

As a crab, you can develop too hard a shell, a good defense for your tender underbelly but one that can lead to isolation. With this placement you'll need to find ways to honor the strength of your vulnerability while developing the healthy boundaries necessary for living a life connected to other messy, loving, and changeable humans.

👁 Affirmations

- Care is my greatest currency.

- Feelings are not facts, but they carry within them kernels of truth that I am dedicated to uncovering.

📝 Reflection Questions

- Where do you feel that your emotional power is most appreciated and put to good use?

- Who do you let take care of you?

- Is developing emotional bonds or initiating others into feeling their emotions tied to your life's purpose? If not, are you known as someone who is attuned to the feeling realm, and is that a central part of your identity? How does that influence others around you?

SUN IN LEO

♌ ☉

In the Northern Hemisphere, where this astrological system originated, the Sun is the strongest in late July and August. The Sun was therefore given dominion over the sign where it produced the most heat. The Sun rules Leo. This is its home, its throne, its place of majesty.

The Sun in Leo has access to all its resources, all its talents, and all its glory. Having the Sun in Leo means that you are meant to burn bright. Confidence, eminence, and heart are some of the positive attributes of the Sun in this fixed fire sign. Here your Sun shines without shame. Gloriously, lavishly, and unabashedly exclaiming itself as the central giver of heat and light, your Sun in Leo needs to celebrate and be celebrated.

Royal in your style, your Sun in Leo needs to rule something. Though not everyone born while the Sun is traveling through Leo will be driven to lead, at the very least your central mission in life is to find a way to give of your life force and get applauded for it.

A Leo unloved can be a dangerous creature.

Humans are attracted to light, and Leo takes that knowledge and runs with it. Leo is the archetypal performer, the clown who steals our heart with warmth and charisma. Passion, love, drama, playfulness, nobility, courage, romance, and exhibitionism are all traits of your Sun in Leo.

When this placement is distorted, it can become egomaniacal, domineering, and self-obsessed. Without the right stage, your Sun can become a bitter, graceless, heartbroken creature whose playfulness gets overshadowed by entitlement. Your Sun in Leo needs to find the most appropriate uses of its charisma and charm so that self-righteousness gets cut off before it can take root. Using your personality as a vehicle for doing the work that is yours to do in the world is where your Sun in Leo will lead you toward great fulfillment.

👁 Affirmations

- I am allowed to love the applause I receive.

- I honor my energy by finding ways to joyfully express it on the stages that are most appreciative of it.

📝 Reflection Questions

- Where in your life do you feel applauded, appreciated, and recognized for your gifts?

- Do you admonish yourself for needing applause and appreciation from others? If so, why?

- Do you feel that your self-expression, creative energy, and ability to shine are tied to your life's purpose? You may still be figuring out the specific way in which you shine, but does the thought of utilizing your creative energy in the world feel important and central to your life's purpose?

SUN IN VIRGO

♍ ☉

In this mutable earth sign that is forever assimilating the knowledge it is receiving, your Sun in Virgo shines through a personality that prides itself on never stopping at "good enough."

You most likely feel invigorated when you've spent time, energy, and effort developing and perfecting the skills you want to apply to your life's work. Never resting on your laurels, your Sun in Virgo will forever be busy refining some aspect of your offering.

Serious in nature, your Sun in Virgo has a job to do and cannot be distracted from it. Varying astrological factors can impact this trait but, in general, you will always feel a greater sense of ease when working efficiently on something that is meaningful to you. Earth signs shine when getting things done that have a tangible result and a practical use. At the very least, anxiety is quieted when distracted with work that bears good results.

Virgo's exacting nature is always attuned to the inner critic. Your Sun in Virgo can learn to dissuade the inner demons of perfectionism if you refocus your awareness on being of service to something you feel is sacred. Being ruled by Mercury means that the mind is forever moving from one topic to the next, and in Virgo's case that can become about searching out one flaw after another.

Not everyone with the Sun in Virgo is an introvert, but this sign pulls awareness toward its own energetic storehouses. Understanding the reserves that you have access to, the reserves that need to be doled out sparingly, and the reserves that are instantly replenished is Virgo's job. Your Sun in Virgo's frayed nerves can often be soothed by cleaning, clearing, and cleansing.

These daily or mundane rituals can become mini rites of passage for you. Putting things in order helps mental, physical, and emotional energy flow.

Virgo's symbol is the virgin, the archetype of individuals who belongs to themselves. Virgo is the priestess, and here the Sun has a talent for understanding the ways of natural healing. Since Virgo is so adept at understanding systems, here your Sun needs you to apply your energy toward what clarifies, specifies, and pinpoints both the problem and the remedy.

When your Sun in Virgo is distorted, you may spend all your energy being hypercritical, micromanaging, and tearing your best efforts to shreds for lack of correctness. Virgo can miss the mountain for the molehill, the love for the flaw in delivery, and the moment for how it thinks it should be. Your Sun in Virgo needs you to find all possible avenues to pour your energy, expertise, and effort into helping yourself feel affirmed by way of being useful.

👁 Affirmations

- I forgive myself. I love myself for being human.

- The most perfect thing I can achieve is my devotion to my process.

📝 Reflection Questions

- How does your inner critic impede you from being able to take action, create, build with others, or be present in your life?

- What are you driven to get perfect? When does that serve you? When does it derail your ability to complete a project?

- Do you feel that your ability to be exacting is tied to your life's purpose? Where in your life does your discernment serve you best? Where in your life does your ability to understand systems of healing help you to understand something about your calling?

SUN IN LIBRA

In this cardinal air sign that initiates relationships, the Sun in Libra strives to find balance between self and other. Between shapes and sounds. Between textures and tones. The Sun in Libra is the Lovable Artist. Relator. Peacemaker. Personable Problem Solver. Diplomat. Activist. As a cardinal sign ruled by Venus, Libra is here to initiate relationships and aesthetic partnerships.

Your Sun in Libra shines by being fair, measured, and willing to meet halfway, always weighing how the other person is feeling, what they are needing, or when they are even the slightest bit off. You shine by being relatable, extending your goodwill, and making life easy for others in times of difficulty. Your Sun in Libra helps soothe any discomfort by addressing the imbalance almost instinctually.

In Libra, the Sun is in its fall, meaning it is in a place that is opposite to where it is applauded and noticed for its courage, strength, and bravery (Aries). Having the Sun in Libra means that you are here to demonstrate that you are a diplomat, fair and even-tempered, and open to all sides of the story, but Libra's dependence on being the receiver of others' affections runs counter to the job that your Sun has set out to do. The Sun is supposed to express itself no matter the consequences.

When the Sun is in a sign that is overly concerned with how others feel, what they might think about you, or how you might find peaceful relations with them, your ability to be boldly yourself, shining as you see fit (the job of the Sun), may be impeded.

Your Sun in Libra will feel every injustice, every slight, every unfair setup—which can sometimes leave you without your own needs met. In pursuit of making a situation seemingly more equitable, do you often lose?

Your Sun in Libra makes you relatable because that is in many ways your job. You attract others through your easygoing nature that most find soothing, if not enticing, to be around. When distorted, your Sun in Libra can be indecisive, people-pleasing, vain, and have a hard time being transparent for fear of having to deal with someone else's upset.

The Sun in Libra offers incredible gifts of balance, harmony, and justice, but you'll need to learn that it is okay to center your own needs in your own life.

👁 Affirmations

- Discord is an important part of growth.

- I can only truly please myself, so I start there.

📝 Reflection Questions

- Where in your life do you allow discord, imbalance, and disharmony to exist?

- What power do you connect to when you feel aesthetically authentic?

- Do you feel that your ability to create beauty, initiate relationships, and maintain harmony is tied to your life's purpose? Where in your life do you feel that relationship building is a bridge to living out your life's purpose?

SUN IN SCORPIO

♏ ☉

The Sun in this fixed water sign shines with a mysteriously alluring glow. Fixed water doesn't flow freely but concentrates deeply. It harbors secrets like currency and holds its energy close, like a good hand in poker. You cannot fool this sign. It most likely knows your motives before you do.

Ruled by Mars, Scorpio cuts through the psychological defenses that harbor the truth. Your Sun in Scorpio shines through a personality that penetrates the emotional, psychological, and psychic realms. It wants to know the secret behind the secret. Like an iceberg, your Sun in Scorpio has an immovable quality. Its depth can't be fully appreciated at first glance. Your Sun in Scorpio will always be more comfortable concealing some aspect of your power until, that is, someone bumps into it. Holding the emotional records of a lifetime, if the icy waters of Scorpio were to thaw out at once, your rising tides could capsize us all.

The fixed nature of this sign means that if you have the Sun here, you'll tend to develop a personality that is not easily swayed. Your power lies in your ability to focus your energy. You may not win in the moment, but you are playing the longest game known to humankind. Your Sun in Scorpio is not going to be impulsive; instead, it is deeply committed to being strategic. This kind of strength and focus gives you a resilience that often intimidates others. Rarely does Scorpio shy away from the gory, the difficult, or the disastrous. Your Sun in Scorpio knows that being connected to the entire experience of life, including death, is regenerative, powerful, and precisely what being here is all about.

The symbol for Scorpio is the scorpion. Scorpions await their prey. They do not hunt. They do not chase every option. They do not waste their time on anything they are not certain of. But once they have set their sights, you can be sure that they will withstand everything from agony to existential dread and boredom to get it.

🦯 Affirmations

- I trust my gut—its messages are a gift.

- My personal transformations are a natural part of my life process.

🖋 Reflection Questions

- Are you often in need of personal transformations to feel vital and alive? What have been your more extreme transformations?

- When you don't have something to call your own, do you tend to control your outside circumstances? How does this show up in your life?

- Do you feel that your ability to demonstrate and use your power, hold appropriate secrets, be investigative, and work in ways that are transformational is tied to your life's purpose? This may not have revealed itself as true at this point in your life, but does the idea itself feel affirming to you?

SUN IN SAGITTARIUS

The Sun in this mutable fire sign knows how to roam. Sagittarius seeks, and with the Sun in this sign, the personality developed is usually one that is philosophical, confident, and optimistic. You are open to experiencing life in all its variations. With Jupiter as your Sun's ruling planet, part of your life's purpose is lived out by going big with whatever you do, and most likely you'll want to do everything at least once.

If something is good, your Sun in Sagittarius will want a lot of it. Most comfortable galloping the horizon, this fire sign is exuberant, operating on faith and copious amounts of information. Jupiter is the planet of wisdom, symbolizing teachers, scholars, and priestesses of all orders. Here your Sun takes on these archetypes and expresses them through the personality.

The symbol for Sagittarius is the centaur holding a bow and arrow aimed at the truth. Your Sun in Sagittarius is that arrow, fired into space, aiming for the ultimate answers to life's deepest questions and on a quest to discover what to believe in and how to uplift and encourage everyone you encounter.

Like all mutable signs, Sagittarius is double-bodied. Half human, half horse, this fire sign is known for needing multiple projects on the go. Moving in all directions, your Sun in Sagittarius may make it so that you have a hard time choosing, but you're also more likely to have the stamina for many things at once. Fire signs have a special knack for knowing when to move on an opportunity. You need the space and autonomy to act on your intuition.

The Sun in Sagittarius can be rash and insensitive. As a fire sign, the need to take action is high but leaves little time for reflecting on how your actions themselves may impact others. This fire sign out of balance always runs the risk of hubris. With Jupiter, planet of exaggeration, as its ruler, the Sun in Sagittarius can get itself into trouble, well-meaning perhaps, but trouble nonetheless. Those with the Sun in Sagittarius will need to find the lanes in life that are theirs to race down and inspire others to do the same in their own way.

👁 Affirmations

- I pause to consider what I might be rushing past.

- My exuberant faith creates my luck.

🖊 Reflection Questions

- Where in your life do you feel free to move at your own pace? Where in your life do you usually overextend yourself? Why?

- Do people often tell you that you are inspiring? What do you think it is that inspires them?

- Do you feel that your ability to embody optimism, faith, and wisdom is connected to your life's purpose? How so? Does your ability to look for solutions or tap into your own energetic well of abundance steer your ability to live out your life's purpose?

SUN IN CAPRICORN

♑ ☉

In this cardinal earth sign, your Sun in Capricorn finds ways to practically utilize your resources. Capricorn wants to make things work. Earthy in sentiment, Capricorn is interested in what will help it reach its mountain peak of choice and is not overly concerned with what won't. Here, your Sun develops a reputation for being a high achiever.

Your Sun in Capricorn is more than likely able to shine while being pragmatic, but it's a pragmatism born from creatively engaging with the tools at your disposal. To do this, you must master the art of restriction. No sign understands long-term gratification like Capricorn.

Capricorn is ruled by Saturn. The slowest planet in the traditional system, Saturn appreciates the gift of time. It takes many Moons to get through a year, and both Capricorn and Saturn innately know how to conserve energy.

Often feeling more comfortable expressing yourself with a little time under your belt, your Sun in Capricorn is a silver fox awaiting its season. "Getting better with age" is a sentiment made for this sign.

With the sea-goat as your mascot, you have the ability to climb any mountain and swim the depths of any sea. Your Sun is most likely captivated not only by the thought of scaling the structures that intrigue you but also by ruminating in the waters of creation. Not always outwardly emotive, you travel to the realm of feeling on your own terms. Mountain goats are solo creatures, after all.

With the ringed planet as your ruler, your Sun in Capricorn is going to be big on boundaries. Self-containment is your Sun's style and your survival tactic. Your rules of engagement should be taken seriously—by yourself and by anyone else who wishes to have your devotion. Others might not know what boundaries you have, but they certainly will know when they have crossed one.

Distorted, the Sun in Capricorn can become rigid, overly skeptical, critical, and harsh. Like its ruler, Saturn, the Sun in Capricorn can become too remote. You may be hard-pressed to connect for the sheer sake of it. This placement isn't likely to have you seeking comfort from others; rather, you may get comfort from adhering to your own personal code of ethics. You might need to learn how to open up to life's opportunities so that you aren't missing out on the fruits of your labor for being so busy cultivating your fields.

☀ Affirmations

- My responsibility is to honor love, joy, and pleasure as much as I honor my work in the world.

- I honor my need for solitude.

✎ Reflection Questions

- What part of you tends to suffer or go without, to achieve the things you most want? Is this necessary?

- What or whom do you feel most responsible for?

- Do you feel that your ability to manifest your creative energy through being consistent, responsible, self-restraining, and reliable is a part of your life's purpose? If you've not yet found your way to do this, does the thought feel resonant to you?

SUN IN AQUARIUS

In this fixed air sign, your Sun expresses its nature by concentrating your energy toward your intellectual pursuits. The Sun in Aquarius helps you to develop a personality that gets you known for your ability to understand and innovate systems to work best for all. The Sun in an air sign will express itself through intellect, communication, and the ability to exchange ideas, but Aquarius is (traditionally) a Saturn-ruled sign, which means it is a little remote. Cool. Boundaries intact. The ringed planet comes with its own mechanism for creating the space it needs.

The symbol for Aquarius is the water bearer that pours forth its libations to humanity. Here the Sun has an incredible gift of unwavering vision. Aquarius is a sign that is adept at intellectual discernment, reserving its exuberance until it understands a situation thoroughly. Its clarity tends to pierce the muddiness of emotionality so that a problem can be solved.

The Sun is in its detriment in Aquarius, the sign opposite to its home in Leo. Here, the Sun has to function in a sign focused on the group, not on its own personal needs. The Sun in Aquarius is usually more comfortable thinking about humanity than having emotional exchanges with other humans (unless something else in the chart runs counter to this). For air signs, the head is generally an easier space to reside in than the heart. The mind is where Aquarius has the greatest strength, yet it can always become a weakness if the rest of the being is not developed.

Just as the Sun struggles in the relationship-centric sign of Libra (its fall), so too in Aquarius (its detriment), the Sun loses strength by not being focused on self-expression. That's not to say that you can't be as powerful or as self-obsessed as the next person, it just means that the focus is on your ability to create structures that foster equality.

The Sun in Aquarius can signify someone who works differently from others. You are not dependent on the attention that the Sun usually seeks out, giving you a possible air of aloofness.

Being the smartest person in the room is perhaps easy for you, but it's also how the distortion of your Sun will tend to manifest. Your Sun in Aquarius can become so logical that you may be tempted to forgo the messages of your heart. Learning to feel, emote, and be in relationship with your physical self can do wonders. Once connected to the wisdom that resides there, you are unstoppable.

👁 Affirmations

- My emotions have their own logic.

- I am allowed to not know what to do, say, or think about a situation.

✎ Reflection Questions

- Where in your life does logic serve you best? Where in life does purely relying on logic hinder your growth? What do you tend to become overly rigid about in your thinking?

- What helps you develop and maintain a connection to your emotional life?

- Do you feel that your ability to understand systems and how to innovate them or that your ability to demonstrate and direct your intellectual abilities is tied to your life's purpose?

SUN IN PISCES

In this mutable, double-bodied water sign, your Sun in Pisces wants to move in every direction. Water without a container soaks itself into the seams of every surface it can reach. Being both moist and mutable makes your personality one that is malleable, sometimes gullible, adaptive, reflective, and illusive. Here your Sun encourages you to develop a personality that gathers influences from as many sources as possible. Your Sun in Pisces cannot help but permeate your environment, giving you the reputation for being compassionate, kind, empathetic, and pacifistic. A natural nurse, healer, artist, and poet, your Sun in Pisces is most likely talented at leaving an impression on the world.

Pisces is a highly fertile sign, and here your Sun shines by being versatile. You are reenergized by having as many experiences, both in and beyond the physical world, as possible. That isn't to say that there is no need for times of rest and deep reflection. Like all water signs, Pisces needs to recuperate the emotional energy it puts out. Like all mutable signs, Pisces might also feel drained from its attention being dispersed too widely.

The symbol for this sign is two fish swimming in different directions, bound by a cord. This symbol encapsulates the paradox at the heart of this persona. Much like two people rowing in different directions in the same boat, Pisces can spend a lot of energy swimming in circles. Perhaps this whirlpool effect eventually leads to another dimension, but the Sun in Pisces is a personality that is often torn, wanting to experience everything, talented at many things, and easily bored by consistency.

Lifelines are far from linear for you. You swim to the rhythm of your own streams, flowing along the currents of your own life rather than following a set path. You may be known for having a mystical, elusive quality. Others might get mad about it, but you can evaporate at a moment's notice. Your Sun in Pisces is a great escape artist.

When distorted, Pisces can end up a martyr, wandering, unstructured, distracted, lost, dazed, and confused. Pisces has a penchant for picking up every stray cat and broken-winged bird. Compassion is the most honorable quality, but without a healthy amount of discernment, it's of little use. If you have the Sun in Pisces, you'll always benefit from learning more about your personal boundaries. That knowledge is vital. It's not your responsibility to heal everyone—or anyone, for that matter.

👁 *Affirmations*

- I reclaim my energy from the world around me.

- Being clear about what I want and need is how I learn to take care of myself.

📝 *Reflection Questions*

- Where in your life does your sensitivity act as your strength?

- Do you tend to get overwhelmed with other people's feelings? If so, what helps you to cleanse and release what you may have picked up from others?

- Do you feel that your ability to empathize with others, demonstrate compassion, and manifest your creative visions is tied to your life's purpose? Do you feel like you are able to utilize your sensitivity or imagination toward something in life that feels fulfilling?

HOUSE OF YOUR SUN
IN WHAT AREA OF LIFE DO YOU
NEED TO SHINE?

What House Is Your Sun In?

Remembering that the planet is the what, the sign is the how, and the house is the where, when we look at what house your Sun is

THE FIRST KEY: YOUR SUN // 67

in, we are looking at the place in your life where you must learn to shine, develop your personality, and perform a part of your life's purpose.

For example, if your Sun sign is Virgo, known for being hard-working, analytical, and thoughtfully precise, and it is in the 2nd House of livelihood, assets, and resources, your life's purpose most likely needs to be lived out through the work you do to support yourself. You'll need to find meaning in your work to feel that you have a purpose. You may be a writer (Virgo is usually quite astute at crafting a sentence) who focuses on social commentary and critique. Or you may be an analyst, a doctor, a healer, or an herbalist. The point is that you need to develop a sense of self (the Sun) in regard to your relationship with money, assets, and livelihood (the 2nd House), by being thoughtful, helpful, critical, precise, and healing (Virgo).

Dr. Angelou's Sun is exalted in Aries (in the sign that gives the Sun strength and possible fame) in the 9th House of travel, education, publishing, and philosophy. The Sun, like each planet, has one house where it is said to be in its joy. The place of the Sun's joy is the 9th House, the house traditionally known as the House of God. Any planet in the place of its joy is in the house where it is happiest and able to do its job with great confidence. This setup—an exalted Sun in the house of its joy—is an especially strong one. It gave Dr. Angelou a confidence, capacity, and vitality with which to blaze a trail in the field of publishing. It is no wonder, then, that Dr. Angelou's first book, *I Know Why the Caged Bird Sings*, completely disrupted popular opinion in the publishing industry that a black woman's autobiography wouldn't be successful. Her debut work unflinchingly spoke to the impact of white supremacy, specifically in regard to slavery and Jim Crow in the American South, and it was also one of the first works to explicitly talk about child rape. It would go on to be a bestseller for two years and remains an integral part of the canon of American literature.

 Now it is time to choose your own adventure. Skip ahead to read the section about the house that your Sun is in.

SUN IN THE 1ST HOUSE

The 1st House is a place of vitality, energy, self, body, and appearance. It is the only house in the chart focused on our own identity; every other house is about another aspect of our lives. Therefore, any planet in the 1st House demands to be an intrinsic part of who we are.

If you have the Sun in the 1st House, you'll have to learn to live out your potential through the vehicle of your personality. By yourself, for yourself. This doesn't mean that life isn't about being in relationships or that relationships themselves aren't central to your life's purpose, but finding a way for your Sun to shine is key. Both the 1st House and the Sun deal with the self and the energy of our life force, so there may be exaggeration or emphasis on self-development if you have your Sun in the 1st House. The self and personality must be lived out through the style of your Sun's sign and any other planets sitting with it. Your Sun is urging you to find all authentic ways to express your solar nature and discover how it can serve your life and its purpose.

Reflection Questions

- In what ways is your personality in service of your life's purpose?

- Are you someone who gets recognition for what you do and who you are (even if it's uncomfortable to you)?

- Do you feel conflict or ease when being witnessed in the world?

SUN IN THE 2ND HOUSE

The 2nd House represents our possessions, our money, our worth, and our property. If you have the Sun in the 2nd House, income, financial resources, property, self-worth, and work are critical to your self-development. With this placement, you'll need to find work that allows you to shine, take up space, and come into your potential. Your identity is an asset that helps you to support yourself. One of the greatest challenges most of us face is finding ways to make an income that doesn't cause greater harm to our world or ourselves. Capitalism flourishes when others and the earth are exploited. Understanding your identity through how you choose to engage, disrupt, or re-invent the exchange of labor and goods may be a central theme in your life. The kind of work you do will depend, in part, on the sign your Sun is in, but no matter the sign, developing yourself through how and where you make a living is critical. This doesn't mean you do or don't make a lot of money. It doesn't mean you do or don't have an easy time supporting yourself. It only points to the area of life where you must learn to take up space in your own way and in doing so understand who you are and what your potential is.

Reflection Questions

- Where in your work life do you feel capable, confident, and purposeful?

- Which of your own sign's qualities do you most want to express in how you make a living?

- How is a part of your life's purpose lived out and expressed via your relationship to your assets, talents, and resources?

SUN IN THE 3RD HOUSE

The 3rd House represents communication, daily rituals, neighborhood, siblings, extended family, and good friends. In motion, we are less stable and more available to the influences of the world. If your Sun is in the 3rd House, you'll most likely thrive in transit and in transitional spaces. Here, your Sun shines while going about your day. With Sun in the 3rd House, you'll need to spend your energy communicating, exchanging, and dispersing ideas, and will generally have a lot going on at all times. Relationships with siblings, cousins, extended family, and close friends will play a key role in the development of your life's purpose. That's not to say these relationships are easy, but the issues that come up within them can become defining for you. Because this is also the house of ritual, and traditionally known as the Temple of the

Goddess, having your Sun in the 3rd House could mean that you have a natural affinity for spiritual ritual, Goddess cultures, mythologies, and religions, or that spirituality is an essential part of your identity.

✎ Reflection Questions

- How much of your day is spent in motion, physically or mentally?

- Do you feel more alive with a variety of things to do every day?

- How much of your day is spent reading, writing, or speaking to others?

- How have your relationships to siblings, extended family, or others defined your sense of self?

SUN IN THE 4TH HOUSE

The 4th House is known as the beginning and ending of all things. This is where we find our roots and traditions. It is the house of parents, grandparents, and ancestry.

With your Sun in the 4th House, you'll have to grapple with an identity that is deeply embedded in your family story—whether that be a positive one or a challenging one. That isn't to say that you'll feel a part of your family of origin or that those relationships are easy for you, but there is a strong connection between your personal development and the family system that you come from. You may work with your family, work at home, or work with other families. With Sun in the 4th House, it becomes important for you to seek out and understand your roots and ancestry. It may also be necessary for you to create and build your own foundation and home.

Reflection Questions

- In what ways do you, or did you in the past, feel comfort or a sense of identity and rootedness from being a member of your family?

- What issues in your family make it hard for you to find your own sense of self?

- What have you learned about detaching from your roots enough to establish your own identity? Is it especially hard for you to do so?

SUN IN THE 5TH HOUSE

The 5th House is a place of pleasure, joy, self-expression, creative projects, children, sex, sexuality, erotic energy, and romance. If your Sun is in the 5th House, you need to find ways to shine in these areas. Having your Sun in the place known for having a good time can also lead to spending a significant amount of your energy seeking pleasure. Others may depend on you to lighten the mood, have fun, and be the life of the party. Some of your life energy may end up distracted by romantic endeavors, games, and whatever entertains you, but what looks like distraction to the outside world might just be your way of working.

 Reflection Questions

- What outlets do you have for your creative energy?

- Does a significant amount of your energy go toward making life better for children? Are you a parent or caregiver to a child or children, and, if so, is that one of the more defining roles you have taken on?

- What do you learn about yourself through spending time developing creative projects or having fun and enjoying life?

SUN IN THE 6TH HOUSE

The 6th House is the house of health and health issues, work, employees, and the problems that arise when our work environments aren't fairly set up. Having your Sun in the 6th House does not mean that you will necessarily encounter health issues or that, if you do, it will be a lifelong situation. You may simply be adept at addressing pain and suffering.

If you have the Sun in this house, you'll need to learn how to find work environments where you can fully shine. You are likely to be highly proficient at what you do and how you do it, so finding the places and people you most want to align with will be key. The Sun is a vital life force, and the 6th House is sometimes a place that makes it a little harder for the light of your Sun to shine. Part of discovering your vitality and life's purpose may have to do with facing, interrupting, and addressing what is systemically oppressive, especially in regard to labor, human trafficking, the legacy and history of slavery, and economic inequity.

Reflection Questions

- What part of your life's purpose is tied to movements for liberation, justice, and equality?

- Do you often find yourself in a supporting role at work? When is this empowering? When is this disempowering? Do you often overwork?

- What do you appreciate about your body? What frustrates you most about it? How are you healing your relationship to it?

SUN IN THE 7TH HOUSE

The 7th House is the place of marriage, committed partnerships, and business relationships. To have your Sun here means that some part of your purpose needs to be lived out in a relationship or in regard to partnerships. You may find that no matter how independent you are, being with others is a main path toward the realization of your potential. Usually with the Sun in the 7th House, life is flooded with committed partnerships of all kinds.

This can look fun from the outside, but often it is difficult to realize your dreams on your own.

 Reflection Questions

- What partnerships have been important in the unfolding of your life's purpose?

- What feedback do you often get from others you are in partnership with?

- Is partnership difficult for you but something you know you need to realize in this life?

SUN IN THE 8TH HOUSE

The 8th House is the house of death, inheritance, mental anguish, other people's resources, and sharing our energy, time, talent, and assets with others. Having your Sun in the house that deals with the psychological pain that comes from loss can make you acutely aware of suffering, both your own and that of others. Therapists, trauma specialists, healers, death doulas, bereavement counselors, mediums, and those who help others cross the waters of our most difficult emotional states often have something significant in this house.

With the Sun in the 8th House, you might have had very substantial losses in your life, near-death experiences, dealings with mental illness, or you might have survived many life events that brought you to the edge of life's limits. These events will tend to shape and reveal the nature of your destiny, drive, and purpose.

On a more practical level, with your Sun in the 8th House, you might find that you are adept at working with the assets, resources, and talents of others with a profitable end for all.

📝 Reflection Questions

- Do you have a talent for taking someone else's skill or resource and molding it into something that they couldn't do on their own?

- Do you feel especially close to the suffering, pain, and loss of others?

- Is a main part of your life's purpose to help hold and create spaces for trauma-informed healing practices?

SUN IN THE 9TH HOUSE

The 9th House is known in traditional astrology as the House of God. Since the Sun was seen as God (and the Moon as Goddess, which is why the 3rd House is the place of the Moon's joy), the 9th House is the house of the Sun's joy. Having your Sun here gives it a special quality and strength. The 9th House is the house of spirituality, religion, philosophy, higher education, publishing, long-distance travel, and long-term plans.

With your Sun in the 9th House, you might need to find ways

to express yourself through exploring the world. Any work that takes you on international adventures or into contact with other cultures and geographies is a natural fit. That said, it's a mistake to think that the Sun here yearns only for physical exploration. It also seeks to travel far and wide philosophically. You might have the qualities (if not title) of spiritual guide, educator, leader, or publisher.

 Reflection Questions

- Does traveling reenergize you? Does it help to connect you to your purpose?

- Was religion or spirituality a major part of your formative years? What negative experiences have you had in organized religion? What positive experiences have you had in churches, temples, mosques, or other places of worship?

- Do people often marvel at your ability to synthesize knowledge? If so, what are you teaching or learning when you feel most aligned with your life's calling?

SUN IN THE 10TH HOUSE

The 10th House is the place of career, public roles, prominence, and reputation. The Sun in the 10th House must manifest itself out in the world. With your Sun here, you must shed your light in places and spaces where it will be seen. There is nowhere to hide in the 10th House. Here everything is public, and either your personality is used as a vehicle for your profession or your identity is tied to roles that you occupy in the world. You may or may not be comfortable in the spotlight, but with the Sun in the 10th House, you must make peace with it at some point, as you'll either be thrust into it or feel a sense of unlived potential for refusing it.

Reflection Questions

- What public roles do you occupy that help you feel a sense of purpose?

- Does public praise seduce you? Do you ever seek it out at a cost to your sense of integrity?

- Do you often find yourself in professional roles where your personality is just as important as the work that you are doing?

SUN IN THE 11TH HOUSE

The 11th House is traditionally known as the house of good spirits and is associated with the fortune that comes from connecting with others. The 11th House is the place of friends, groups, associations, allies, community, and those who share the same hopes and dreams as you. With your Sun in this house, you'll get where you're going in life through those whom you know. Friends, groups, and social events are very important for you. The more you place yourself in the company of like-minded people, the faster your trajectory and discovery of your life's purpose. Having the Sun in the 11th House tells you that there are beneficial connections for you to make. The more you seek out common goals with others, the more you'll notice that those who can help you get there are ready and willing to do so.

📝 Reflection Questions

- Do you feel that your life's purpose is, in part, lived out by your connections to communities, friends, and patrons? How have you "lucked out" by knowing the right people or being in the right place at the right time?

- Do you feel energized by being connected to others who share the same visions for the future as you do?

- Do you have difficulty in groups but find that you are always placed in them or that they are important to achieving your life's purpose?

SUN IN THE 12TH HOUSE

The 12th House is the house of sorrows, self-undoing, loss, incarceration, institutionalization, the collective unconscious, hidden life, secrets, behind-the-scenes work, and the deep well of creative energy that is available only when we are engaged in healing our deepest wounds.

Here, your Sun may want you to work with those who are or have been incarcerated or who are struggling with any kind of mental, emotional, spiritual, or physical illness. With the Sun in the 12th House, it's important to spend time understanding how pain and suffering work. Studying what keeps humanity bound in sorrows will also lead you toward what unlocks our creative potential. The Sun in the 12th House can develop a deep respect for the human condition and how we might ultimately get to our own liberation. There are no quick fixes here, only a deep process of transforming lead into gold in the cauldrons of our soul. This is also a place in the chart that can't be seen, so with your Sun here, you may need to spend a lot of time in solitude, in secret, or in the darkrooms of creation.

✍ Reflection Questions

- Do you tend to shine in dark rooms, studios, creative incubators, or meditative spaces? Do you need time in such environments on your own to recharge and tap into your creative energy?

- Has mental illness, loss, incarceration, and the suffering of others been an important part of your work in the world?

- Do you tend to have a knack for picking up on what others need, what will be relevant, or what will be popular?

RELATIONSHIPS WITH OTHER PLANETS
WHO IS IMPACTING YOUR ABILITY TO SHINE?

Which Planets Are in Aspect to Your Sun?

In astrology, as in life, everything is influenced by relationships. Aspects are relationships between planets. Some aspects will encourage your Sun to flourish with ease (the sextile and trine—the "gifts"), while others will set up significant obstacles on the path to self-realization and self-acceptance (squares and oppositions—the "challenges"). Sometimes it all depends on which planet is involved (as is the case with conjunctions—the "mergers").

In many astrological texts, aspects are called "witnessing," as in one planet bearing witness to another. If someone witnesses us, they can tell others about us—for better and for worse. What might it mean for our Sun to be witnessed by its astrological nemesis? Saturn will scrutinize us, Venus will see our best, Mars will notice our weaknesses, and Neptune will fantasize about who we could be.

Planets conjunct the Sun make themselves known through the personality. They demand to be merged with one's identity. The Sun, the self, cannot be expressed without the significations of any planets that conjunct the Sun. Conjunctions can be helpful or challenging depending on the nature of the planet. Mars and Saturn will challenge, Venus and Jupiter will help, Mercury is usually neutral, and Uranus, Neptune, and Pluto are a mixed bag.

Staying with Dr. Angelou's chart, we see that her Sun is conjunct both Jupiter, planet of optimism, abundance, and prosperity, and Uranus, planet of innovation, rebellion, disruption, and change.

Further evidence that Dr. Angelou's chart has an astrological mark of success is found when examining her Sun exalted in the place of its joy and conjunct Jupiter, a planet that has the ability to offer the blessings and protection of exuberance, optimism, wisdom, and generosity. When I see a planet in a chart that has this many advantages, I take note. It was of course up to Dr. Angelou to shape this successful signature into something that would be meaningful for her, as is the same for all of us. However, we can see that from birth, she had direct access to the gifts that she was meant to give forth. Rather than become embittered by life's circumstances, which would have been completely understandable, Dr. Angelou became an artist, activist, and educator whose work held a mirror up to white supremacy, reflecting back the origin of the problem to itself. Jupiter's significations of overcoming hardship through faith in one's ability to be bigger than cruel-hearted, oppressive forces is perhaps best encapsulated in Dr. Angelou's famous poem, *Still I Rise*, an ode to her work as both an artist and an activist.

Her Sun also sits within 10 degrees of a conjunction with Uranus, the Awakener, the Radical, the Rebel. This aspect is illuminated by Dr. Angelou's involvement with many social movements and civil rights actions in her lifetime. Throughout her entire life, she carried with her an ability to disrupt apathy, injustice, and harm with her direct and thoughtful messages as well as with consistent and unglamorous work. Before she was a celebrated author, Dr. Angelou was an artist and organizer. She was director of Martin Luther King Jr.'s Southern Christian Leadership Conference, worked directly with Malcolm X as a cofounder of the Cultural Association for Women of African Heritage, and documented the anticolonial struggle while editing the *Arab Observer* when she lived in Cairo.

Sun conjunct Uranus might be considered as harmful as it is

helpful, however. Being so disruptive, Uranus's flare for being inventive may not be appreciated until we've learned how to navigate its eccentric path. It speaks to the wild twists and turns Dr. Angelou's life took, and how unconventional a person she was, but it also speaks to the chaos she experienced as a young child being moved about many times between her mother and grandmother.

 Now it is time to choose your own adventure. Look back at the list of aspects to your Sun that you wrote down on page 39 and read the sections that apply. Then skip ahead to the reflection questions at the end of this chapter (page 94).

Gifts

SEXTILES

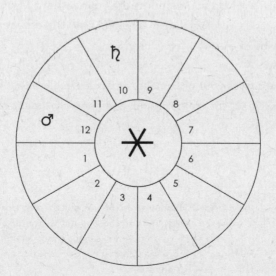

The sextile is a 60-degree angle that is friendly and mild but helpful and encouraging.* A sextile from any planet to your Sun will be beneficial, even if subtle.

A sextile from your Sun to . . .

- **Moon** creates a harmonious relationship between your soul's purpose and your way of living it out.

- **Mars** will instill your identity with courage and energy. It will generally promote your ability to find your way through life, unfazed by what most might fear.

- **Jupiter** will encourage an optimism and faith in life. This aspect magnifies your ability to create opportunities through your own enthusiasm and acts as a blessing to you personally.

- **Saturn** will help you demonstrate your authority, your boundaries, and your discipline in a helpful way. This aspect gives you the vibe of a boss.

- **Uranus** gives your personality an eccentric flare that helps you get noticed, speak your mind, and generally find it easy to be different.

---

*Venus is never more than 48 degrees from the Sun and therefore cannot technically sextile it. It can be two signs from the Sun but will never be a full 60 degrees from it. For this same reason, Venus cannot trine, square, or oppose the Sun. Mercury cannot be more than 28 degrees from the Sun and therefore cannot sextile, trine, square, or oppose it.

- **Neptune** lends a dreaminess, glamour, and imagination to your personality. This aspect can promote your ability to connect to others through compassionate understanding.

- **Pluto** creates depth, intensity, and an undeniable power. This aspect can help you connect to influential people.

TRINES

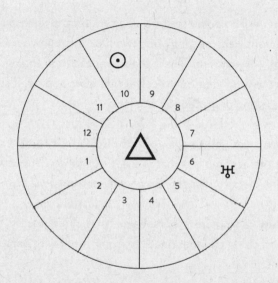

The trine is a 120-degree angle that is harmonious and helpful. Stronger than the sextile, trines are able to impact a person's life in more definitive ways. Trines from any planet to your Sun will encourage your talents and gifts. Quite often we take these gifts for granted, as they are easy for us. When we haven't worked for something, we often diminish its value. When we are having a hard time, however, if we focus on the trines in our chart and the blessings they bestow on us, we can more easily get back on track.

A trine from your Sun to . . .

- **Moon** creates a harmonious relationship between your soul's purpose and your way of living it out.

- **Mars** will make taking risks and demonstrating your strength and courage look easy to the outside world. This aspect helps you to care for and defend what most needs it.

- **Jupiter** will help you to show up in an expansive, inspiring, and exuberant way, creating your own luck through your faith that things will work out. This is the strongest trine that any planet can receive; if your Sun receives one from Jupiter, it signifies a certain kind of protection and luck.

- **Saturn** gives you the gift of self-discipline, structure, and the ability to accomplish what you set out to do. This aspect creates an identity that thrives when achieving goals.

- **Uranus** can create a personality that finds it easy to break with tradition and that needs to experiment with personal self-expression.

- **Neptune** grants a heightened sensitivity, a vivid imagination, and an easy and relaxed demeanor that others find magnetic.

- **Pluto** creates depth, intensity, and power, and can also help you to attract influential people.

Challenges

SQUARES

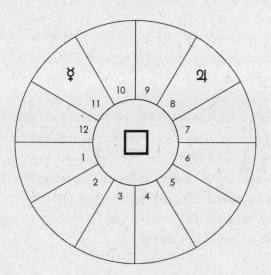

Squares to our Sun occur when there is a planet 90 degrees to the left or right of it. Squares cause tension, aggravation, and action. They can lead to emotional, mental, and possibly physical discomfort. However, this discomfort is dynamic and can cause the person to take much action to alleviate the discord.

A square from your Sun to . . .

- **Moon** will give you a desire to act. In general, the Sun and Moon in a square aspect give you a feeling of inner tension that drives you.

- **Mars** is a challenging aspect that may create violence, anger, and aggression. Yet when reckoned with, you can become adept at working in situations that others are too afraid to tackle, or at channeling your energy into courageous action.

- **Jupiter** will generally veer on the side of optimism and exuberance but can exaggerate your ego, persona, and belief in your own skills and abilities.

- **Saturn** can feel like an obstacle that depresses your life force. Responsibilities may be cumbersome, and internal or external critics can inhibit your path. However, working through these obstacles will bring the best of you to the fore. Developing compassionate discipline and being dedicated to building a meaningful life can liberate you from the more oppressive manifestations of this aspect.

- **Uranus** can cause disruptions either to you or through you, and it often challenges the status quo (for better or for worse). This signature will create a personality that is shocking or contrary. This can feel positive, necessary, and exciting to you and others, as well as unnerving.

- **Neptune** can lead to self-deception and a blurring of boundaries, making it difficult to be consistent, grounded, and realistic. However, working with the sensitivities and artistic talents that Neptune usually brings can be a positive way to tune into and use this very otherworldly energy.

- **Pluto** can confront you with experiences of loss of control, abuse, and struggle for autonomy and your own power. This aspect usually creates a very deep and introspective nature. You are someone who, if you chose to heal from your more harrowing Pluto experiences, is comfortable plumbing the depths of the psyche and soul. The kind of personal power this creates in you is undeniable.

OPPOSITIONS

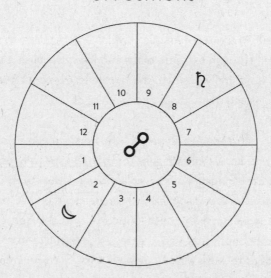

An opposition to your Sun occurs when there is a planet in the opposite sign. The opposition is exact when the planet is 180 degrees away. Oppositions challenge us, force us to confront things, and push us to strike a balance even in difficult times.

An opposition from your Sun to . . .

- **Moon** means that you were born just before, during, or just after a Full Moon. You need to fully express your potential in the world through the development of important partnerships and creative cross-pollination.

- **Mars** can make you feel like you have lost your power, energy, drive, and ambition through experiences that are psychologically or physically harmful. To balance this out, you need to learn how to deal with your own anger, how to manage conflict with consciousness, and how to protect yourself from harm when and where possible.

- **Jupiter** can create a dynamic in which you regularly overextend yourself through extreme highs and lows. Because it's Jupiter, which is naturally positive, the hurdle is less about challenging obstacles and more about the dangers of excess.

- **Saturn** can set up a dynamic where it feels like you are at odds with an authority figure (or many), especially one that is patriarchal. Finding ways to reclaim your authority through disciplined efforts and applied skill can help overcome the feelings of inadequacy, shame, self-criticism, and self-consciousness that this opposition can create. All difficult Saturn aspects get easier to work with as we age, since Saturn demands maturity.

- **Uranus** can bring disruptive life experiences, breakdowns, breakups, traumatic events, and also breakthroughs that change the course of your life. Something exciting, eccentric, or experimental needs to be integrated into your personality.

- **Neptune** can challenge you with experiences that result in a loss of personal boundaries, energy, and vitality. Anxiety, depression, and a loss of direction are common, especially in early life. This is an aspect that can make you want to choose escapism over responsibility, fantasy over reality, and illusions over what is in front of you, all as a coping mechanism. Integrating your sensitivities can in turn help you to develop psychic or artistic talents, an understanding of others' pain, and an astute awareness of the interconnectedness of all things.

- **Pluto** connects you to sources of power that can feel overwhelming. Pluto being the God of the Underworld tells us about what happens out of public sight. Crime, abuse of power, and secrecy are all themes that a person with Sun and Pluto in opposition may be up against. Either you have those experiences yourself, are drawn to investigate what is taboo, or come up against many extreme life events. You need to learn how to work through obsessions and your desire to control life, instead channeling that energy into work that feels deep, cathartic, and transformative.

Mergers

CONJUNCTIONS

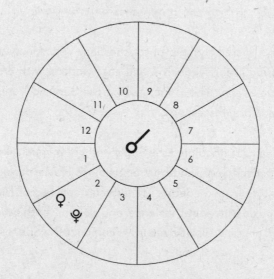

A planet is conjunct your Sun when it is in the same sign as your Sun. It results in a blending of energies. This energy can be positive or negative, depending on the planet involved.

Your Sun conjunct . . .

- **Moon** means you were born just before, during, or after a New Moon. This placement makes you act on your own instincts and will either feel like you have done this before (if born just before a New Moon when the Moon is in an earlier degree than the Sun) or like you are completely new at this (if the Moon is at the exact same degree or a later one than the Sun). Both placements have to rely on their intuitive responses to life.

- **Mercury** is common because Mercury can only be a maximum of 28 degrees from the Sun. This combination can create a clear and consistent channel between your sense of self and the style in which you communicate to the world.

- **Venus** is incredibly helpful for the Sun. Venus lends the Sun a pleasing likability, charm, and ease working with erotic and creative energy. This is increased if the Sun and Venus are in Taurus, Libra, Pisces, or Leo.

- **Mars** can be difficult for the Sun to integrate, much like Saturn conjunct the Sun. The positive attributes of Mars are courage, vitality, drive, and energy. The difficult qualities of Mars have more to do with anger, violence, and wounds, both psychological and physical. If you have Mars conjunct the Sun, one of the main obstacles to living your purpose is to accept that part of your purpose is to be controversial. If you can learn to channel your competitiveness toward what's helpful, you will go a long way. This is a little more of a seamless placement for those with Sun and Mars in Aries, Scorpio, and Capricorn.

- **Jupiter** is incredibly helpful for the Sun. The enthusiasm of someone with Jupiter conjunct the Sun is almost impossible to quell. Optimism, vitality, exuberance, and positivity infuse your personality, and you are philosophical, always looking at the big picture. These traits are more pronounced if the Sun is in Sagittarius, Pisces, Cancer, Leo, or Aries.

- **Saturn** means that your persona may lean toward pessimism. This planet's penchant for doom and gloom can be the rain cloud that obscures the Sun's desire to shine brightly and boldly. However, it also lends you the ability to make frank and honest appraisals of a situation. It's important for you to find meaningful work that you can dedicate yourself to. Saturn tends to be unfairly harsh, and with this combination, you may have to learn to cut yourself some slack, otherwise nothing is ever good enough, including you. This combination usually means that you need to temper your judgments with compassion for yourself and others. This combination gets easier with age, as you find your way toward mastery and self-sufficiency. It's also easier in Capricorn, Aquarius, and Libra.

- **Uranus** can create a personality that is exciting, unpredictable, erratic, innovative, and eccentric. Because Uranus spends about seven years in a sign, everyone born with the Sun in that sign will have this aspect. This is why I choose to consider it a dominant aspect of the personality and life only if the Sun and Uranus are within 10 degrees of each other and in the same sign.

- **Neptune**, when within 10 degrees of the Sun, can create a loss of self, since Neptune diffuses anything that it touches. Incredibly porous, you may feel an overidentification with others (or others with you) and a need to work on personal boundaries. Incredible sensitivity needs to be channeled into work or projects that help you connect with what feels larger than you. Spirituality and addiction, recovery, healing, fantasy, art, and dreams can play a part in shaping your life's purpose.

- **Pluto**, when within 10 degrees of the Sun, creates an intense personality that wants to control. Eventually, when this combination learns to transform what is difficult into what can be used for fuel, it is unstoppable. You may need to investigate many aspects of life that are related to the underworld. Accumulating resources can become an obsession if you mistake inner power for outer wealth.

Reflection Questions

- Which planets are helping your Sun to shine? Do you feel their good graces? Do you ever downplay these gifts or take them for granted? How can you support yourself in making the most of this ease in your chart to live out your full potential?

- Which planets are impeding or challenging your Sun's ability to shine? Is it validating to learn this about your chart? How can you support yourself in understanding these challenges as growth edges, not immovable obstacles?

- What have you learned about your Sun that you need to radically accept in order to live out your life's purpose?

IV

THE SECOND KEY
YOUR MOON

Your Physical and Emotional Needs

The Moon has always been an evocative, mysterious source of inspiration for humankind. The second brightest light in our sky, the Moon is our ever-changing nocturnal guide. Astrologically, it represents our needs, wants, and cravings. It represents our changing emotions, our body, the body of the person who birthed us, how caregivers cared for us, and the stories of our past and lineage.

Just like the Moon in the sky, the Moon in our chart reflects the light of our Sun, our life's purpose. It tells us how we live out that purpose in the physical realm. It speaks to our daily experience of manifesting our spiritual selves. It is the reflection of our soul's experience in our body.

Unfortunately, understanding this without judgment is often difficult because we live in a culture that judges our bodies. Living within white supremacy, and the sizeist, ableist, misogynistic, cisnormative, transphobic, classist culture it creates, we are often convinced to degrade our body. Capitalism profits from our rejection of our body, convincing us to invest our life energy, our money, into buying products to change ourselves.

Understanding more about the Moon in our chart can help us give meaning to some of the more difficult experiences we have in our body, perhaps even helping us to have a deeper appreciation for it.

As with the Sun, there are three main characteristics of your Moon that you should consider as you unpack the physical and emotional conditions you need to live out your life's purpose:

1. The sign that it is in (how you meet your physical and emotional needs)

2. The house that it is in (where you meet your physical and emotional needs)

3. Other planets that are talking to your Moon (who is impacting your ability to meet your physical and emotional needs)

Once we are old enough to meet our own needs, it's up to us to find the nourishment we crave. The Moon tells the story of what we need and how we need it. Knowing this can help us to radically accept who we are and take better care of ourselves. If your Moon is in an air sign, it will crave connection, conversation, relationships (romantic or otherwise), and intellectual stimulation. If your Moon is an earth sign, it will need to build something of substance, work in ways that garner tangible results, and have material and physical comforts. In water signs, the Moon needs emotional nourishment, to cry, to have a place to express its feelings and create emotional connections. The Moon in a fire sign will need action, adventure, and passionate exchanges on a daily basis.

Key Points to Remember about Your Moon

- Your Moon represents your physical and emotional needs, your history, your relationship to nurturing and being nurtured, and your relationship to your parent or main caregiver. The Moon is the body that is home to the soul as it lives out its purpose.

- The Moon in your chart speaks to your physical, daily experience.

- It is through the Moon that we unpack our life's purpose daily.

- The sign that your Moon is in, the house that your Moon is in, and aspects that your Moon makes to other planets in your chart will give you important information about how you like to live out your days, what activities you need to do daily, and how to best take care of yourself on a regular basis.

SIGN OF YOUR MOON
HOW DO YOU MEET YOUR PHYSICAL AND EMOTIONAL NEEDS?

What Sign Is Your Moon In?

The sign that your Moon is in will tell you the style in which you emote, get your needs met, build connections, and live out your

CHECK IN WITH YOUR CHART

FINDING YOUR MOON

Look for this glyph ☾ *in your chart.*
This is your Moon.

What sign is your Moon in?

My Moon is in the sign of _____.

What house is your Moon in?

My Moon is in the _____ **house of** _____.

ASPECTS TO YOUR MOON

When you pull up your chart through the CHANI app or at www.ChaniNicholas.com, you will see which planets are in aspect to your Moon. Remember, you may not have any planets talking to your Moon. Don't worry about what the different aspects mean for now. Just note them, and we will dive into their meaning soon. Fill in the blanks below that are applicable to you.

The planets in the same sign as my Moon are _____.

The planets that are trining my Moon (four signs / 120 degrees apart) are _____.

The planets that are sextiling my Moon (two signs / 60 degrees apart) are _____.

The planets that are squaring my Moon (three signs / 90 degrees apart) are _____.

The planets that are in the opposite sign from my Moon are

_____.

daily life. It also points to how you experienced your parents and caregivers. Even though there are psychological properties associated with each sign the Moon is in, it's important to remember that the Moon doesn't have the same strength in every sign. Some signs are more difficult for the Moon to be in, some neutral, and some lend it great comfort.

Frida Kahlo had her Moon in Taurus, the sign of its exaltation. Here, the Moon needs to build something lasting, well-crafted, and sensually pleasing. Because the Moon is in a sign it does so well in, we know that it has the ability to bring about the life's purpose with some confidence and recognition.

As a Venus-ruled sign, Taurus is known for have a penchant for jewelry. Venus loves to be adorned. The fixed earth sign is a lover of rocks, crystals, and all stones that catch the eye and offer grounding. Often laden with massive rings, necklaces (Taurus rules the throat), and earrings, Kahlo was clearly living out her Moon in Taurus (with a flair befitting of her Leo Ascendant). Kahlo used clothing and jewelry as a way to articulate, explore, and remind the world of both her indigenous and colonial ancestry, often mixing statement pieces from both. In addition, Kahlo's body (the Moon) and what happened to it was more often than not the subject of her work and sometimes even her canvas. Because the Moon also represents the home, the fact that hers has been turned into a museum of her art seems fitting for a Taurus Moon that likes things that are built to last.

 Now it is time to choose your own adventure. Skip ahead to read the section about your Moon sign.

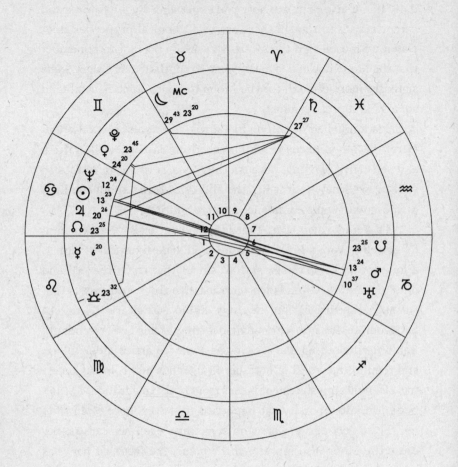

FRIDA KAHLO'S BIRTH CHART

Birth Date and Time: July 6, 1907, 8:30 a.m.

Location: Coyoacán, Mexico City, Mexico

MOON IN ARIES

♈ ☾

The Moon in the cardinal fire sign of Aries is action-oriented. Daily life will most likely be adventurous. Taking action may be a form of self-care. Taking initiative may be a way of helping you feel safe in the world. Taking on challenges is necessary for you to feel vital and alive.

With this placement, independence and freedom are a must to feel emotionally centered, though the level of independence you need will vary greatly depending on the rest of your chart. Regular release of excess heat can be important for your emotional well-being. Feelings can flair but not permanently, as Aries is quick to change.

With this placement, it is common to have had a hot-tempered, independent, or courageous parent or caregiver. Someone who wasn't reliant on others for their sense of self and encouraged you to be the same, or someone who felt a little too fiery to get close to in the ways that you may have needed.

👁 Affirmations

- I honor my need for independence.

- I honor my need to compete with my personal best.

📝 Reflection Questions

- Is risk-taking and adventure part of how you live out your life's purpose?

- What did you learn about channeling, expressing, or working with anger from your parents and caregivers? What did you learn about being independent? What did you always want to do, or end up doing, on your own?

- When does competitiveness get you into emotionally difficult situations or encourage more separation than you'd like? Is that usually coming from you or others? When does competition feel healthy and inspiring of your personal best?

MOON IN TAURUS

The Moon is exalted in Taurus, meaning it has extra strength here and is able to do its job well—nurturing, building bonds, conceiving, and birthing (literally or metaphorically). In Taurus, the Moon needs stable, reliable comforts. Taurus needs to build, and the Moon is good at doing so in relationships, at home, and in all things that bring a sense of security. Taurus isn't a sign concerned with the abstract; it loves the literal. The Moon in Taurus needs sensual pleasures and will turn to them in times of insecurity and emotional instability.

Like all planets that are exalted, the Moon in Taurus helps you to become well-known for your ability to manifest your talents on the physical plane. Incredibly sturdy, here the Moon is on solid, fertile ground. Planets in their exaltation will tend to get attention for their ability to perform their duty. Here, the Moon is productive, giving, and generative. A Moon that others rely on. Lean on. Come to for sustenance. Flattering perhaps, but this Moon needs to learn not to be the feeding trough for every hungry heart.

The Moon in a Venus-ruled sign (Taurus and Libra) knows

how to create connections. In Taurus, this is done through a slow and steady development of the partnership. Reliability never runs out with Moon in Taurus.

You may have experienced a parent or caregiver as strong, sturdy, stubborn, or controlling. Someone who was famous or infamous in their own right. Someone who prioritized security and consistency above all else.

☀ Affirmations

- I honor my need for stability, security, and consistency while encouraging myself to take thoughtful risks.

- I know that my strength is something that others find soothing, but that doesn't mean I have to give them more than I have to spare.

✎ Reflection Questions

- Do you often get the feedback that you are a support system for others? If so, is it ever at your own expense? Does being grounded, or perceived as strong, mean that others don't ask you what you need?

- Did you have a parent who was especially grounded, reliable, or stubborn? In what ways have you adapted or inherited these traits? Which work for you? Which hinder you? Why?

- Do you tend to need to build something, work on something in a consistent way, or apply yourself to something tangible when you feel insecure or adrift? Is doing so a part of how you live out your life's purpose? What are you currently working on that feels aligned with your Moon in Taurus?

MOON IN GEMINI

♊ ☾

The Moon in Gemini needs to communicate, process, and exchange the facts and ideas that it is constantly gathering. It needs to access many different avenues of information. Needs to ask questions. Needs to be in a constant state of learning, moving, and transgressing intellectual boundaries.

The Moon in Gemini creates safety and belonging through being conversational, soothes itself through learning (this is the more introverted side of Gemini) or communicating (the more extroverted side of Gemini), and needs to tap into both intuition and logic. You need both introverted and extroverted experiences to regulate but may feel compelled to be constantly in contact with others as a way of feeling safe.

With your Moon in Gemini, you may have experienced a parent or caregiver as more intellectually expressive than physically or emotionally so. They may have been charming, intelligent, chatty, difficult to rely on, or inconsistent.

👁 Affirmations

- I honor my need for a wide variety of relationships.

- I honor my need to intellectually understand my emotions while not dissociating from the feeling of them.

Reflection Questions

- Do you find that when you feel uncertain, insecure, or ungrounded in any way, learning something or having a good conversation helps you regulate? If so, what kind of information feels the most soothing to you?

- Do you often need to explore a diversity of options, relationships, and interests to feel like your needs are being met? How is that related to your childhood or upbringing? Is it part of how you live out your life's purpose?

- Was one of your parents especially curious, intellectual, sociable, or duplicitous? How has that impacted you?

MOON IN CANCER

In Cancer, its own sign, the Moon feeds the masses. Here the Moon is strong, extreme in its significations, and undeniable in its power. The Moon in Cancer needs to nourish others as much as others need its nourishment. To feel safe in the world, Moon in Cancer develops emotional bonds, in many cases ones that feel like family. Security comes through connection to others but can also come at a cost. This Moon can lose itself in the role of the caretaker, forgetting that its own needs are as valid as anyone else's.

Extremely sensitive, empathic, and intuitive, you will pick up on, and most likely hold, the unprocessed emotions of others. Learning to release the energy that you have absorbed from others is a lifesaving tactic.

Moodiness is often the marker of having lost one's emotional boundary. To regulate, you will likely need a safe place to call home, a shell to crawl back into, and a sanctuary in which to cleanse yourself of the residue of human suffering.

Since the Moon is in its place of power, there may be an experience of ease or abundance on the material plane, especially in regard to the house that it is placed in. Because this is such a dominant placement, you may also feel more resonance with your Moon than your Sun. Issues related to the Moon in general (feeding, caring for, caring about, bonding, writing, and moving about the world) may feature prominently in your life.

With this placement, it is common to have experienced a parent or caregiver as extremely nurturing, comforting, or emotionally suffocating. A Cancer Moon can indicate a parent or caregiver who was a very dominant figure in your development. We can say this about all caregivers, but if you have a Cancer Moon, you may feel particularly tied to the lessons and teachings you received from them.

👁 Affirmations

- My needs are just as valid as anyone else's, and I take thoughtful care of my spiritual, intellectual, and physical self.

- It's okay to outgrow my past.

📝 Reflection Questions

- Where in your life do you feel you have the most confidence or natural talent? In the next section, see if it relates to the house that your Moon is in.

- What care do you tend to give others? Is it part of how you live out your life's purpose?

- Was one of your parents an especially strong figure in your life? If so, how were they significant to your development? How were their emotional needs overwhelming to your system?

MOON IN LEO

♌ ☾

The Moon in Leo needs attention, applause, appreciation, and acknowledgment in its daily life and experience. It needs to express itself creatively and take inspired action. It might be hard to regulate your own self-esteem in earlier life without an audience, but learning how to appreciate and applaud yourself is necessary.

Your Leo Moon needs to shine, making part of the learning process about finding the best stage for your star. There is a quality of being special to this Moon, and that is alluring to many, but not every kind of celebration is good for the soul. If you were shamed or made to feel that you were merely attention seeking in early life, you might have developed a complicated relationship to attention, attracting it unconsciously and being unsure of what it means when you receive it.

You might also feel guilty or uncomfortable for receiving the praise that you do, as it's not something you necessarily have control over but is something that you need. Some with this placement can become addicted to the sensation and emotional stimuli of being praised. You may be good at garnering the attention, but without it you can feel a loss of self.

You live out your daily life with a confident style; even if you don't feel confident, you will present with an emotional strength most times. However, you need to turn away from the audience occasionally and make sure that you are being true to your own story.

You might have experienced a parent or caregiver as exciting, glamorous, celebrity-like, overbearing, egomaniacal, or self-absorbed. You may need to reclaim your self from the overwhelming personality of your parent or caregiver, particularly if they had a fiery temperament that manifested as both creatively inspiring and too hot to touch.

👁 Affirmations

- Applause is something I need, but I seek my own approval first.

- I am lovable and deserving of attention, no matter who is watching.

📝 Reflection Questions

- Are you someone who has a natural talent for making people laugh, putting them at ease, or getting attention for the things that you do? How do you feel when this happens?

- Are you naturally open to leading and shining in the positions you take up? Is it part of how you live out your life's purpose?

- Was a parent or caregiver especially dramatic, glamorous, or in need of applause? If so, how did this make you feel?

MOON IN VIRGO

♍ ☽

The Moon generally does well in Virgo. Comfortable in the coolness of this earth sign, in Virgo the Moon nurtures life and others through being of use. It creates safety and belonging by working hard, learning, developing its skills, being of service, digesting information, and analyzing data. Virgo needs to clean, clear, organize, purify, and have things in proper working condition as a way of emotionally regulating. A little decluttering of the mind, body, or home can go a long way for the Moon in Virgo's nervous system. A Virgo Moon needs ritual. It may or may not need to be consistent, but the process of refining anything can be soothing to this soul.

Because this Moon is adept at critique, if and when that energy gets turned in on itself, or those around it, the results can be disastrous. Virgo distorted will tear things apart in search of a solution, ending up with nothing but hurt feelings and an overly scoured system.

You may be obsessed with trying to find perfection, denying yourself the right, and the beauty, of being human. Learning how to channel this energy toward skill development and the rituals that keep you cleansed of self-criticism is your life's work. Since Virgo is so attuned to what doesn't work, your Moon is especially adept at understanding the rhythms, systems, and ways in which healing naturally occurs.

You may have had a parent or caregiver who was health conscious, well-versed in the healing arts, introverted, overly critical, or unable to accept themselves. If the latter is the case, you may want to consider how this has impacted your own sense of self.

👁 Affirmations

- I am allowed to make mistakes, learn, and try again.

- My emotions don't have to be understandable to be acceptable.

📝 Reflection Questions

- Do you have a habit of trying to fix, adjust, or change yourself when something outside you isn't working? Was there a parent in your early life who was critical of you, or were there others who made you feel like you had to adjust yourself to avoid their critique?

- What special gifts do you have for understanding herbs, natural ways of healing, healing modalities, or different ways of cleansing the mind, body, or emotional system?

- What do your gifts for editing, eliminating, organizing, writing, and communicating bring you? Is it part of how you live out your life's purpose?

MOON IN LIBRA

The Moon in Libra needs to create beauty, bring peace, or partake in the pursuit of justice daily. This Moon is acutely aware of when things are out of balance. The discord of injustice is felt deeply. Part of its self-soothing strategy is to put things back into a harmonious relationship. Be that with colors, sounds, textures, words, or in partnerships with others, this Moon provides the emotional temperament of a peacekeeper.

You are adept at establishing connections, making others feel witnessed, and extending yourself out to those in need. You get your needs met, in part, by being likable. However, when your emotional needs are reliant on being in partnership with others, you can experience a lot of anxiety when necessary and needed conflict arises. You might be so sensitive to disagreements that you contort yourself into all manner of shapes to compensate.

Having a difficult time confronting the people you love is par for the course with this Moon. So is feeling plagued when faced with the need to choose between options, people, or main courses at dinner. Reminding yourself to prioritize your needs above all else should be a daily practice.

You may have had a parent or caregiver who had a hard time dealing with confrontation, someone who was overly concerned with appearances, or who was extremely likable and social. You might have also learned how to be pleasing to make up for their lack of tact.

☼ Affirmations

- Disagreement is part of the peace process.

- I focus on my needs as a way of being a better partner to everyone in my life.

📝 Reflection Questions

- What helps you remember that conflict is a necessary part of life?

- Where in your life do you seek justice as a daily practice? Where in your life do you create beauty as a daily practice? Is it part of how you live out your life's purpose?

- Did you have a parent or caregiver who was averse to discord, taught you to be "good" or "nice," or was graceful and easy to be with?

MOON IN SCORPIO

♏ ☾

The Moon seeks comfort, stability, and security. It likes to be in a sign that facilitates a sense of grounding and ease. It wants to settle in and celebrate the mundane. Scorpio yawns at such simplicity.

In the intense, extreme, and resilient sign of Scorpio, the Moon is in its fall. This doesn't mean that life in and of itself will be difficult, but you will called on to dig deep and transform your pain into purpose.

The Moon in Scorpio unpacks its soul's purpose in ways that might evoke intense emotions, creating bonds with others that are deep, transformative, and possibly possessive at times (either you are or others are with you). When distorted, this Moon can become fixated on maintaining control instead of finding ways to compost difficult emotions to allow for new experiences.

You have the ability to move through difficulties, work through emotional intensity, and face extreme situations with a greater ease than most. You innately understand all manner of abuses, misfortunes, and difficulties, lending you an incredible depth, sensitivity, and emotional endurance.

This Moon may represent a parent who was emotionally powerful, overbearing, manipulative, strong-willed, resilient, resourceful, magnetic, or a combination of all of the above. Because Scorpio deals with death, loss, and transformation, sometimes having the Moon in this sign speaks to not only experiencing these issues in childhood but also having them as part of your professional interest or expertise.

👁 Affirmations

- My depth of feeling is a resource that can teach me how to have compassion for others.

- I honor my intensity; it is a wellspring of creative energy that I can channel in a million different ways.

📝 Reflection Questions

- What helps you to process your more intense emotions? How does your need to maintain control impede your ability to do so?

- Are intense emotional experiences part of how you live out your life's purpose?

- Did you have a parent or caregiver who had an especially difficult time or who was dishonored or disrespected in some way?

MOON IN SAGITTARIUS

The Moon in Sagittarius seeks what it needs with bravado. It takes care of itself by taking action. It nourishes itself by pursuing the truth.

The Moon in Sagittarius needs adventure. It is comforted by travel, leaps of faith, new ideas, philosophical study, and anything that helps it feel expansive, alive, and in motion.

Its optimism makes you resilient. You survive by searching for the best in people, places, and situations. You connect to others through positivity and need to feel like you are growing and developing every day.

If your Moon is in Sagittarius, you'll function well when you allow yourself to be led by your inspirations, insights, and intuition. You may be extreme in your emotional responses and feel the need to take off in a direction before you have really understood the consequences, especially if you are trying to avoid something.

You might have had a parent or caregiver who was a scholar, traveler, adventurer, or free spirit. You may have experienced them as too distracted by bigger things to be interested in your needs as a child. Having your Moon in Sagittarius can sometimes point to parents or caregivers who were extreme in their ideological or religious beliefs.

👁 Affirmations

- I expand my options every time I listen to my intuition.

- I believe in the abundance of my life.

Reflection Questions

- Does traveling, learning, and doing things that are spontaneous help you regulate emotionally? Is it part of how you live out your life's purpose?

- Do you feel safest when you also feel free? What does it mean to you to feel free? When do you feel unfairly limited or restricted?

- Did one of your parents or caregivers feel larger than life to you, know a great amount, or need a lot of freedom? What meaning did you make of that when you were young?

MOON IN CAPRICORN

Here, the Moon creates safety and security through accomplishing tasks, climbing to new heights and proving itself as a responsible, reliable, productive member of society.

Capricorn Moons might do their due diligence before they do self-care, but like any other placement they can learn otherwise. As a way of establishing security in life, Moons in Capricorn will work harder than expected, putting in consistent effort until they feel depleted (though their stamina may be legendary).

Extremely self-reliant, Capricorn Moons feel safe when in control of their situation. Austere and diligent, this Saturn-ruled sign can use self-denial as a coping mechanism, and in some cases as a way to care for themselves. You may go without in order to feel good. Restraint may feel rewarding but must be balanced with a keen understanding of what you need to give yourself.

You might struggle to find connections that feel easy. A sense of lack can permeate, especially in early life. Emotional and physical comforts might feel unsatisfying or be missing completely. Because the Moon rules the physical self, you may have a hard time in your body, connecting to your body, or nourishing it.

Boundaries are important to your Moon. Emotionally speaking, there may be parts of you that few to zero people get a glimpse of, but the ones who do will be sacred to you. With an acute awareness of the bleak and grim realities of life, you might have an incredible sense of humor and deal with painful and delicate emotional material in very practical ways.

You might have had a parent or caregiver who was too burdened with responsibility or tradition to be able to care for you. The work of a Capricorn Moon is to understand where malnourishment occurred, so that there can be a repair of harm and a replenishing of whatever the lack in early life was. Whether you have parents or caregivers who were responsible, reliable, and accomplished, or too out of touch with their own emotional life to be able to recognize yours, you need to learn to replace constraint with comfort, whatever that means for you.

👁 *Affirmations*

- I am committed to being kind to myself.

- I pause to replenish myself whenever I feel empty.

Reflection Questions

- What do you feel guilty asking others for? Is this a feeling that you experienced in childhood or with a parental or authority figure? How can you support your own healing of this?

- Is being pragmatic and driven toward accomplishing tasks a central theme of your life?

- Was one of your parents or caregivers overly burdened with responsibilities or unable to meet your emotional needs? What meaning did you make of this?

MOON IN AQUARIUS

The Moon in Aquarius needs space. Here the Moon is fed by learning, communicating, and understanding the systems we live within, how they work, and how best to innovate them.

This Moon needs to be understood and intellectually challenged to feel emotionally safe. Creating security through detachment, the Moon in this sign needs to find logical conclusions to the problems of the heart, and logic is hard to reach when it is embroiled in emotionality. Distance is needed if this Moon is ever to sort itself—and the solutions it needs—out. An incredible stubbornness can set in with this placement, creating difficulty in being fluid with the ebbs and flows of emotional life. Others may experience you as emotionally remote, but none should mistake your Moon's style for a lack of feeling. The emotions are there, even if nowhere near the surface. Feelings aren't facts, but they do lead you to your truth.

The Moon in Aquarius wants to find solutions that work for all involved and can often leave its needs on ice to achieve a kind of equality. But nothing can be fair when you are forcibly denying your feelings. Your work is to learn how to create space for your own emotional experience and to value your body, heart, and soul as much as your mind and intellect.

You may have had a parent or caregiver who was intelligent, emotionally reserved, cool, or driven by needing things to be a certain way.

☯ Affirmations

- I am open to the wisdom that comes when I am able to sit with how I feel.

- I give myself the space I need.

▤ Reflection Questions

- Do you tend to push others away when your feelings are overwhelming?

- Do you feel that your life's purpose is lived out, in part, through your ability to manifest your intellectual talents?

- Was one of your parents or caregivers known for their intelligence or emotional reservedness? What meaning did you make of that? What did they teach you about working through difficult emotions?

MOON IN PISCES

♓ ☾

Your Moon in Pisces wants to help you live out your life's purpose through implementing the power of your imagination, sensitivity, creativity, and compassion in your daily life. Your Moon will imbue the mundane with either a fantastical sensibility or a deeply empathetic one—which is, in part, how you meet your emotional needs and create safety. Moon in Pisces wants to either merge with others or escape when the situations get sticky. This can be frustrating for others who felt so witnessed by your understanding ways. Here, your Moon wants to reflect to others their feelings and beauty, but it balks at any and all restraints on its ability to make a move. The fish is good at swimming, not always at staying still.

With this placement, it is often too tempting to escape the confines of daily life. Your Moon will most likely do well in the environments that encourage your intuition, sensitivity, imagination, and creativity.

As a way of protecting yourself, you might space out, check out, or peace out when others least expect it. Music, movement, art, creativity, and any healing work or endeavors help you channel your Moon in Pisces. Your Moon might need many ways to manifest its talents during the day. Pisces always wants a smorgasbord of opportunities and delights. This Moon wants those kinds of options daily.

Incredibly empathic and tuned into the suffering of others, you may get lost in the pain that you feel from the world around you. This Moon can act like a healing balm to many, but often to its own detriment. Your boundaries are the best attribute to beef up on. Helping others means you need to know where you begin and end.

You may have had a parent or caregiver who was extremely creative, sensitive, and caring, emotionally dependent on you, or prone to martyrdom. Parents and caregivers with addiction and mental health issues might also have been present in your childhood.

👁 Affirmations

- I honor my boundaries, giving what I have in excess and keeping what I need for myself.

- I can tune into the pain of others while releasing it from my system.

✐ Reflection Questions

- What helps you to keep your center and not lose your sense of self when those around you are in pain?

- How does your sensitivity serve the unfolding of your life's purpose?

- Did one of your parents or caregivers have difficulty with substance abuse or mental health, or show a great gift for being creative and intuitive with the needs of others?

HOUSE OF YOUR MOON
WHERE DO YOU MEET YOUR PHYSICAL AND EMOTIONAL NEEDS?

What House Is Your Moon In?

The house that your Moon is in is where you find comfort, where you get fed, and where you need to connect in a meaningful way with your life's purpose. The house that your Moon is in is one of the most important areas of life for you to understand, live consciously into, and develop your relationship to. Since the Moon comments on parents and caregivers, the house that it is in can speak to something regarding your childhood, the person who birthed you, and your lineage.

With an exalted Moon in Taurus, in the 10th House of career and public roles, Frida Kahlo had one of her key planets at her professional aid. Set to work in the area of her life that was the most visible, her exalted Moon in the 10th House helped her to secure a place in the world for herself, despite many substantial odds. Just having a planet in its exaltation has the ability to bless the house that it is in and its significations will be brought about more easily. The way in which Frida Kahlo needed to live out her life's purpose and find emotional and physical comfort (the Moon) was through building and securing (Taurus) a body of work that would become a monument and testament to her life (the 10th House). As mentioned earlier, Frida Kahlo's home was both the place in which she created most of her works of art, and it has also become its own museum. The pain and beauty of her physical existence (the Moon) was the most common theme of her work, and her career was one of the places in her life that granted her some ease and much success.

Now it is time to choose your own adventure. Skip ahead to read the section about the house that your Moon is in.

MOON IN THE 1ST HOUSE

The 1st House is the house of identity, self, body, appearance, vitality, character, and strength of spirit. As one of the most prominent houses in the chart, having your Moon in the 1st House makes the Moon a very active planet in your life.

This placement can heighten your sensitivities, making you a natural nurturer. Feeding others emotionally, physically, and spiritually will most likely be second nature to you. Here, the Moon can create a personality that reflects others back to themselves. This can be an intense or calming experience depending on the sign that the Moon is in, but it is alluring either way.

In constant exchange with those around you, the Moon in the 1st House wants to give and receive information. Highly responsive to environmental conditions, here the Moon is impressionable, moody, and changeable. Having the Moon in the 1st House means that part of unpacking or living out your life's purpose will be through developing yourself.

Reflection Questions

- Are you someone who wears your emotions on your sleeve?

- Do you get the feedback that others feel reflected, witnessed, or comforted by you?

- Do you tend to focus on your appearance when you feel out of sorts, uncomfortable, or insecure?

MOON IN THE 2ND HOUSE

The 2nd House is the house of livelihood, assets, moveable resources, self-esteem, and self-confidence.

Having the Moon in the 2nd House means that you need to unpack and live out a part of your life's purpose by understanding how to successfully work with your resources, inner and outer assets, money, property, and issues of self-worth.

Here the Moon wants to create security through developing resources and maintaining them. You might find that you need access to, or need to be engaged in the development of, material comforts in order to feel secure and safe enough to thrive. Your work may have something to do with fertility or infertility, conception, women, gender-nonconforming folks, femmes, caregiving, nourishing others, child care, the Goddess, writing, or communicating.

📝 *Reflection Questions*

- What role does the development of your resources play in your life's purpose?

- What was your parents' relationship to money when you were a child? What is your first memory of money?

- Does your work have to do with the body, reproductive health, caregiving, Goddess culture, or writing? If so, what do you find that you are particularly skilled at in these areas? When was the first time you realized it?

MOON IN THE 3RD HOUSE

The 3rd House is the house of siblings, extended family, communication, daily rituals, short-term plans, local travel, and neighbors. It is also known as the temple of the Moon or Goddess. The 3rd House is the house of the Moon's joy, making the Moon especially strong in the 3rd House. Here the Moon helps you connect to a great many people, ideas, conversations, rituals, and spiritual practices or sentiments. This placement wants you to live out your life's purpose by writing, teaching, learning, or working with divinatory practices.

Movement might be an important aspect of living out your life's purpose, with teaching, circulating information, and providing care and nourishment to others as part of your daily routine. You may need a lot of mental stimulation, information, and data, especially when you feel insecure or unsure. You may also have important relationships with siblings, extended family, and close friends with whom you share familial-like bonds.

📝 Reflection Questions

- Do you live out your life's purpose through what you write, speak, or teach?

- What role do your siblings, cousins, extended family, and good friends play in your life?

- Did you or do you act as a caretaker or a parent for a sibling?

MOON IN THE 4TH HOUSE

The 4th House is the house of home, family, caretakers, parents, and grandparents. The 4th House is the foundation of our lives, the beginnings and endings of all things.

With your Moon in the 4th House, you need to live out your life's purpose by creating a foundation for your life. The family that you come from may or may not be a place of refuge for you, but creating such a space is of paramount importance. Since both the Moon and the 4th House are interested in and oriented toward our history and the past, you may be particularly skilled at studying or understanding ancestry, origin stories, and history. Often when the Moon is in the 4th House, it can speak to having an interest in working with families, people's homes, real estate, or in the domestic realm in general.

Reflection Questions

- How does being close to family (chosen or not) factor into your sense of well-being? What in your life tends to go a lot better when you feel connected to a group of folks that feel like family?

- Is your ancestry something that you study, work to develop a relationship to, or something that you feel connected to? How does that show up in your life, work, or relationships? How does the study of your lineage factor into your life's purpose (or how might it)?

- What part of your work involves families, home environments, housing, or has to do with the literal or symbolic foundations of life? What about this work are you naturally good at?

MOON IN THE 5TH HOUSE

With your Moon in the 5th House—the place of children, creativity, fun, leisure, sexuality, and erotic energy—your life's purpose needs to be lived out within some aspect of these domains of life. Because both the Moon and the 5th House have such a strong association with conception, reproduction, sex education, and the birthing process, anything to do with these areas of life may be second nature to you, or may be especially challenging, important, and life-defining for you.

However, human reproduction isn't the only kind of creativity that the 5th House cares about. The creative process, creative energy, creative projects, love affairs, pleasure, and leisure activities are also central to how you live out your life's purpose with this placement. Creative disciplines may help you connect to a sense of purpose, as well as to channel moods and emotions.

This placement sometimes reflects having a parent or caregiver who was influential in the lives of children or focused on any of the other significations of the 5th House, including art, pleasure, and creative self-expression.

☑ Reflection Questions

- How is creative energy and its expression central to living out and unpacking your life's purpose? What happens to you when you have somewhere to put your creative energy? What happens to you when you don't?

- How is reproductive health or sex education an important part of your life's purpose? What talent does working with children or youth help you to access? What does being a parent, caregiver, or mentor to the children in your life help you to fulfill or understand about yourself?

- What do you need to make, create, or work on when you feel insecure, unsure, or disconnected from your life?

MOON IN THE 6TH HOUSE

The 6th House is the house of work and health issues. When we struggle through an illness or have chronic pain, we don't have the same kind of energy or ability to do what we want when we want to. Physical discomfort demands that life be lived in a certain way, a way that the world generally makes even more challenging. With your Moon in the 6th House, you may be sensitive to or experience issues regarding accessibility, injury, illness, and physical suffering.

The 6th House is also the house of work, work habits, and the tools that we have to do the jobs we must (which can involve livestock and small animals, making this also the house of pets). Having your Moon here can speak to your experience or knowledge of economic injustice and systemic power imbalances in the workplace. The 6th House represents the situations where we aren't in charge—which is neither a positive nor a negative in and of itself, but not having full autonomy is a theme of the 6th House.

However, what houses like this can teach us about life is invaluable. Not having the kind of access to resources that makes life easy or accessible is a central experience to most people on the planet. In the 6th House we can learn how to accept the aspects of life we have no power over and redirect our energy toward where we do have agency. Being open to the truth of our lives means being acutely aware of the precariousness of it.

If your Moon is in the 6th House, part of your life's purpose may need to be lived out through work-related projects in general. The Moon in the 6th House can be soothed by a job well done, being of service, taking care of pets or animals, working through health issues, learning different healing modalities, or understanding illness and its causes.

Having your Moon here might mean that you have been impacted by a parent, caregiver, or family member's experience of a health issue. This placement may also want to nurture those whom you work with or for. You may do work that is caretaking, work in the domestic realm, in people's homes, from home, or work that requires emotional labor or emotional intelligence.

Since this is the house traditionally associated with slavery, work that unpacks its history and impact or that addresses human trafficking, worker's rights, and fair labor conditions can also be part of your lived experience.

Reflection Questions

- Do you work with or find meaning in serving those who live with illness, chronic or otherwise? Do you work in ways that promote healing and care for those who experience pain? Does any part of your work involve worker's rights, trafficking, or the modern or historical impact of slavery? If so, what about this work are you naturally adept at? What brought you to the work? What keeps you there? How is your mental, emotional, and spiritual health as a result?

- Is part of your life's purpose lived out in your work life in some meaningful way? What does your work help to facilitate for you?

- Did a parent or caregiver have a physical issue or have to work excessively in your childhood? What did that experience teach you or give you an understanding of?

MOON IN THE 7TH HOUSE

In the 7th House of committed partnerships, romantic, platonic, or professional, the Moon helps to unpack your life's purpose through connecting to others. You'll find that your most important and life-changing experiences occur through intimate relationships and business partnerships. This placement can make you very reflective in partnerships and give you the tendency (depending on the sign it is in) to morph into the people you are with or over-give to them. Emotional boundaries are of paramount importance to develop.

With this placement, those you form close bonds with and decide to commit to can lead you to pivotal experiences to explore, understand, and develop.

✍ Reflection Questions

- Do you tend to look to relationships to give life a sense of purpose, direction, or meaning? When you feel lost, unsure, or untethered, do you turn to committed partnerships to be consoled? Does that ever mean you stay in relationships that aren't totally right for you? What helps you leave partnerships that aren't working?

- Do you feel as though many of the major events in your life come through your partners or partnerships? Which have been the most impactful?

- Did your parents or caregivers often get lost in their relationships? How did this impact getting your own needs met?

MOON IN THE 8TH HOUSE

With the Moon in the 8th House—the place of collaborations and other people's money, assets, and resources—your life's purpose needs to be lived out by learning how to share resources, how to give what you've got, how to receive what you need and how to produce work with others. If you have inheritances of any kind, what you do with them, or how they impact you, will also be important to your life's purpose.

The Moon in the 8th House may understand the process of death and all things to do with the soul's journey after leaving the body. The grief, loss, and mental anguish that can come with the impermanence of life are also found here. This placement can be especially experienced with mental health issues and may be very adept at working with folks who have them or who are working through grief. With your Moon in the 8th House, you may have had a parent who experienced mental illness or worked in the field, or you may have suffered a significant loss that marked your childhood.

The Moon in the 8th House may need to confront emotionally difficult situations and may often go through cathartic experiences. You may also be connected to souls who have left the body. Channelers, psychics, and those who are in touch with the spirit world can often have strong 8th House influences.

Reflection Questions

- Are your collaborations an important part of living out your life's purpose?

- What do you feel you understand about grief and the grieving process?

- What are you sensitive to in regard to mental health issues, loss, and healing the mind? What have you or your parents/caregivers struggled with in regard to mental health? How has therapy or other healing work helped you to address these issues, and has the process revealed something to you about your purpose?

MOON IN THE 9TH HOUSE

If your Moon is in the 9th House, you will need to live out your life's purpose through teaching, traveling, publishing, philosophy, advocacy, spirituality, religion, or pursuing higher education. You may be fed by or find solace in wisdom traditions and through seeking things that feel far off, adventurous, and exciting. In this house, the Moon needs to experience the unknown, needs to be placed in situations where its mind is stretched, where its comfort is challenged, and where it is asked to experience life through a different lens than it is used to.

You may be a very nurturing teacher or have teachers who are more like a parent or play out parental roles, both difficult and desirable. You are an instinctual learner, talented at absorbing ideas and intuiting answers, and have a knack for working psychically with divination practices.

With the Moon in the 9th House, you need to move around, study, work with teachers, work in publishing, or teach others when you feel insecure or unstable.

Reflection Questions

- Do you tend to distribute or need to absorb information when you feel unsure of yourself? Which wisdom traditions do you turn to when you feel off-center? Does traveling or teaching help you feel connected to your life's purpose? What is it about doing either that makes you feel that way?

- Is publishing, in any of its iterations, central to your daily life? What does it feel like for you when you release information out into the world, to a group of people, or as part of your work?

• Was religion or spirituality a big part of your childhood or important to a caregiver or parent? Was this a positive, negative, or more neutral experience? What role does it play in your life now?

MOON IN THE 10TH HOUSE

If your Moon is in the 10th House, you live out your life's purpose through career, social status, and reputation. This Moon wants to achieve social recognition as a way of feeling secure and wants to be recognized by "the people," achieving goals as a way of self-soothing. As a result, people with the Moon in this house sometimes seek fame, or end up with it, without having to make as much effort as others.

This Moon is able to read or intuit the needs and wants of others. The Moon in the 10th House may have a natural affinity for working with the body, birth, and conception, or supplying nourishment in physical, emotional, or spiritual ways. Traditionally this placement was linked to working with water and all things pertaining to bodies of water.

With your Moon in the 10th House, you need to work as a way of taking care of yourself, which can be tricky when you need to rest. You may need to accomplish something professionally as a way of emotionally regulating and will most likely need to watch the ways in which you tend to over-give to the world.

📝 *Reflection Questions*

- When you feel unsure, insecure, or out of sorts, do you tend to work toward accomplishing goals that will garner you more success and recognition? When is this counterproductive, draining, or challenging to manage on a physical level?

- Does getting recognition for your efforts come easily to you? Do others often comment on the kind of attention you receive? What are the comments generally speaking about? Are others often envious of your accomplishments? If so, how do you deal with that?

- Is one of your parents or caregivers well-known or famous in some regard? Did you feel like they were larger than life when you were young? How did this impact your own sense of self?

MOON IN THE 11TH HOUSE

If your Moon is in the 11th House of community and good fortune, part of how you live out your life's purpose is through the connections you build to friends, groups, and possibly through the activism you embark on with them. In the house of good fortune, the Moon nourishes others, and in doing so, creates its own luck. Through building with those who have the same hopes and dreams for the future, you can make at least some of your dreams a reality.

In social settings, group work, and at networking events, your Moon feels a sense of security. You most likely have a strong urge to bring a vision to fruition with like-minded individuals. This is where you thrive, and prioritizing your need to be in community will bring you tremendous joy.

✍ Reflection Questions

- Do you get nourished by spending time or investing in the communities and groups that you are associated with? Do you feel like your connections with others often lead you to important life events? Does this seem to happen naturally, or do you consciously encourage it? If you do, how so? If you don't, how might you?

- Does community organizing connect you to your life's purpose? At the moment, what does that look like? What would you like it to look like?

- Did a parent or caregiver connect to the world through their groups and associations, have friendships as a key component of their identity, or struggle in group situations? How did that impact you?

MOON IN THE 12TH HOUSE

The 12th House represents what is hidden from view, secret, and unknown to our conscious awareness. Those with the Moon here may be drawn to unpacking the secrets of family, culture, and society. With the Moon in the house of hidden projects, part of how the life's purpose gets lived out may be by doing behind-the-scenes work and projects in private, by being in studios, in dark rooms, or in places of isolation that also serve as creative incubators.

This Moon may need time alone to process emotions. Your self-care system might require you to retreat and refuel.

Because this part of the chart also speaks to sorrows, loss, self-sabotage, self-undoing, and all the aspects of self that we tend to want to forget, refuse, or put out of sight, the Moon in the 12th House speaks to one's experience with suffering. This may be inherited from the parent or caregiver, symbolic of their struggle, or in the family line.

Self-sabotage might be a common survival strategy, as paradoxical as that sounds, but eventually the Moon in the 12th House needs to learn ways to heal the past so it can access the incredible creative wealth that gets bound up by unacknowledged pain.

The 12th House is the part of the chart that deals with incarceration, isolation, and institutions, which may be a part of your direct experience or that of your parents or caregivers. You may have an ability to get into places and do important work where others are incarcerated, locked away, or removed from society.

Reflection Questions

- What roles do creative incubators, dark rooms, studios, and places of solitude have in living out your life's purpose?

- Are you comfortable or talented at working with those who have suffered great losses?

- Do you have a parent or caregiver who deals with mental health issues, has worked in or been in an institution, or works with those who have been treated unfairly by the systems they live within? If not, have you?

RELATIONSHIPS WITH OTHER PLANETS
WHO IS IMPACTING YOUR ABILITY TO MEET YOUR PHYSICAL AND EMOTIONAL NEEDS?

Which Planets Are in Aspect to Your Moon?

Just as there are planets in relationship with your Sun, so too might there be planets in relationship with (in aspect to) your Moon. These aspects also fall into the same categories that we explored earlier—gifts, challenges, and mergers. The same theory applies to all planets. Sextiles and trines are helpful gifts that, when in aspect to the Moon, can help you create physical abundance, experience comfort, or cultivate blessings. Squares and oppositions are challenges that can inhibit your access to material and emotional safety, at least at some point in your life. Conjunctions (mergers) can go either way, depending on the planet in question.

Frida Kahlo's exalted Moon in Taurus in the 10th House sextiles her exalted Jupiter (planet of abundance) in Cancer in the 12th House. Since the Moon rules Cancer and is therefore in charge of this Jupiter, there is a special affinity between them that is heightened because they are in a helpful aspect to each other (the sextile). Although the 12th House is a place often associated with great difficulty and isolation, her Taurus Moon was able to translate and bring those 12th House experiences into the 10th House of career. Her ability to express her personal suffering, loss, and experiences of isolation in her art brought her great recognition. It should be noted that if other planets had made challenging aspects to Frida Kahlo's Moon, her career may not have been a place of such great distinction for her.

 Now it is time to choose your own adventure. Look back at the list of aspects to your Moon that you wrote down on page 100 and read the sections that apply. Then skip ahead to the reflection questions at the end of this chapter.

Gifts

SEXTILES

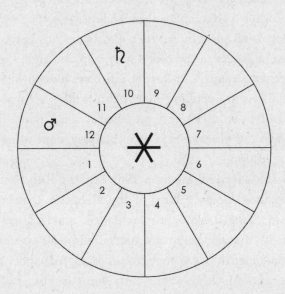

The sextile is a 60-degree angle that is friendly and mild but helpful and encouraging. A sextile from any planet to your Moon will be beneficial, even if subtle.

A sextile from your Moon to . . .

- **Sun** tells us that there is mutual support between the two lights in your chart, and your life's purpose gets unpacked and lived out in a more harmonious way.

- **Mercury** lends a connectivity to your communications, making you naturally perceptive and relatable. A parent or caregiver may have had these same traits.

- **Venus** lends a sweetness and an ability to form bonds that can be of great assistance to you. Venus can also help to beautify your body and home. A parent may have been beautiful and handed down their charm or artistic talent to you.

- **Mars** lends courage and drive to the way you live out your life. A parent or caregiver may have been a role model for a positive kind of protection.

- **Jupiter** lends you a sense of abundance and faith in the way life unfolds, helping you to create and enjoy material and emotional comforts. A parent or caregiver may have been especially buoyant, optimistic, or spiritual.

- **Saturn** creates an aptitude for structure, stability, and discipline to be incorporated in your daily life in ways that feel supportive to your material and emotional well-being. A parent or caregiver may have been good at being a fair authority figure.

- **Uranus** lends innovative insights, a need to shake things up, and a quirky sensibility. With this aspect you might need your days to be diverse, exciting, and always changing. A parent or caregiver may have been eccentric or unusual in a way that was inspiring.

- **Neptune** lends you a vivid imagination and a need to experience emotional closeness. This aspect can heighten your intuition and ability to connect with a wide variety of folks. A parent or caregiver may have been creative or ideal in some way.

- **Pluto** lends you emotional depth, a desire to have cathartic experiences or relate to people in ways that feel transformative. A parent may have been powerful or influential.

TRINES

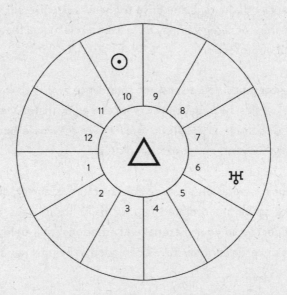

Harmonious and helpful, trines (a 120-degree angle) to the Moon will assist it in ways that support your emotional and physical needs with greater ease. The trine is stronger than the sextile and therefore brings more powerful blessings.

A trine from your Moon to . . .

- **Sun** creates reciprocity between your life's purpose and your way of living it out.

- **Mercury** creates a talent for connecting with people in an emotional way. A parent or caregiver may have been a good communicator or able to express emotions well.

- **Venus** is exceptionally helpful and lends a lot of beauty, likability, charm, and ease to the Moon, helping it to live out life with great style and grace. A parent or caregiver may have been, or may be, attractive, accommodating to others, or at ease in social settings, garnering attention and admiration.

- **Mars** helps you to feel comfortable in a leadership role, taking initiative, going your own way, and supplying yourself with what you need. A parent or caregiver may have been independent, inspiring you to be so as well.

- **Jupiter** is incredibly helpful and lends your Moon a special protection, abundance, optimism, spiritual nature, generosity, and faith in life and getting your needs met. A parent or caregiver may have been generous, optimistic, and able to offer you abundance on the material plane.

- **Saturn** lends you authority in a way that doesn't feel overbearing to others. People may instill trust in you and your integrity. A parent or caregiver may have held an important position or was able to demonstrate how to be mature in ways that didn't feel oppressive.

- **Uranus** helps you to be unconventional in ways that others accept, enjoy, or appreciate. A parent or caregiver may have been experimental, inventive, and creative in their approach to life.

- **Neptune** creates a very intuitive kind of creativity and imagination and may need nourishment that comes from images, sounds, and colors. A parent or caregiver may have been especially intuitive, receptive, or giving.

- **Pluto** can create an emotional intensity, power, and influence that others respond to. A parent or caregiver may have been powerful in their impact on you or on the world around them, connecting you to material blessings.

Challenges

SQUARES

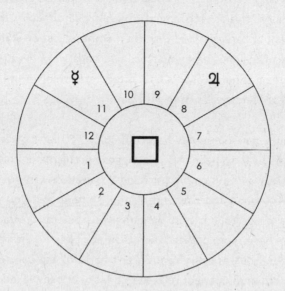

Squares (90 degrees) that the Moon makes to other planets point to places where we might have been, or felt, unsafe physically, emotionally, or materially. Difficult aspects made to the Moon can also speak to inherited or historical trauma as the Moon represents the body and the lineage we come from.

A square from your Moon to . . .

- **Sun** speaks to friction between your life's purpose and living it out. This can mean that your Sun and Moon, two of the key planets in your chart, express themselves in ways that are so different they cause friction in your life, but they also cause you to take action. Paradoxes in your personality are never boring.

- **Mercury** can create a challenge when communicating your feelings. This aspect may also speak to a difficulty that your parent or caregiver had with their communication style, which may or may not have impacted you negatively. A square from Mercury is not an aspect that is too concerning in and of itself, unless Mercury is sitting with Saturn or Mars.

- **Venus** can sometimes have difficulty getting its needs met, since pleasing people is the biggest problem for this planet. There may be a conflict around a parent or caregiver's need for attention and the kind of nourishment that you received as a child. Your parent or caregiver's beauty or charm may have been more present than their ability to take care of your needs. Squares from Venus aren't harmful, but can speak to a discord or disconnect related to beauty or being liked.

- **Mars** can be especially painful, since it has a tendency to be cruel and piercing. This may indicate a parent who had difficulty controlling their anger and may say something about how that kind of behavior impacted you as a child. This aspect needs an outlet for its anger, energy, and drive, and benefits from activities that are cooling and anti-inflammatory for the body, mind, and spirit.

- **Jupiter** can create a need for abundance, overindulgence, and an appetite for emotional experiences. Sometimes a parent was larger than life, exaggerative (emotionally or otherwise), or had a big personality that dominated their child's experience.

- **Saturn** can create stiffness, heaviness, and lethargy in the body or in the emotional system. Depression is a common side effect of a difficult Saturn/Moon aspect. The parent or caregiver of a person with this aspect may have been overly burdened or unable to give nourishment. You can work with this aspect by being disciplined and finding ways to be kind and compassionate with yourself.

- **Uranus** disrupts the foundations of our lives. Often people with this placement feel that their childhood bonds and nurturing were disrupted in ways that felt unsafe. You need to create some source of consistency in your life through building and nurturing bonds.

- **Neptune** creates a tendency to escape life's demands. This setup may speak to a parent or caregiver who had issues with addiction or was not able to be present, was disassociated, or was checked out in ways that made you anxious. You need to learn how to ground yourself and hold your emotional responses without checking out.

- **Pluto** creates very intense emotional reactions to anything that feels unsafe to you. This may have created power struggles with your parent or caregiver such that your own autonomy was threatened. You may feel devoured by your parent's emotional needs. Finding ways to work through and honor your own emotional responses and understanding the intelligence that is inherent in you is both helpful and healing.

OPPOSITIONS

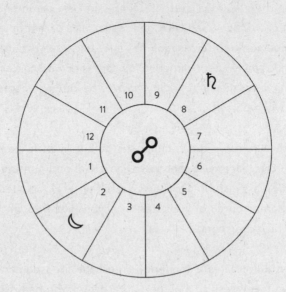

When the Moon is in an opposition (180 degrees) to another planet, it can speak to a split that we have between our emotions and another part of ourselves. It points to something that might have felt like a threat to your security or well-being when young.

An opposition from your Moon to . . .

- **Sun** means that you were born just before, during, or right after a Full Moon and there is a need to integrate the opposing natures of your Sun and Moon signs and placements.

- **Mercury** may find it helpful to balance the needs of the body and mind, may vacillate between head and heart, and may tend to overthink instead of feeling. This placement may also speak to a relationship with a parent or caregiver where balancing rational and emotional interactions is challenging.

- **Venus** may make it difficult to integrate and balance your own needs within relationships. You may feel like your parent or caregiver chose their erotic self or life over your needs. You may need to bring these different aspects of self into balance to welcome and honor both.

- **Mars** punctuates the heat and harm that your body may have experienced. With this placement there is often an adversarial dynamic with others. You need to learn how to protect yourself and may need to channel combative energy into fighting for something noble. A parent or caregiver may have trespassed your boundaries, caused you harm, or perhaps was harmed in a way that impacted your sense of security.

- **Jupiter** has the tendency to exaggerate, over-give, and overdo things in relation to the body, emotions, and connections with others. This is not a "challenging" aspect but requires that you find balance, emotionally and physically. Boundaries may be your biggest learning curve. Over-giving or overestimating what you are physically and emotionally able to offer and then overcompensating in the other direction to come into balance may be a pattern to watch out for. A parent or caregiver may have been larger than life, someone whose personality or needs dominated your world, or someone whose exuberance was exhilarating but not necessarily realistic.

- **Saturn** is the most challenging of all oppositions from the Moon. Having Saturn opposing your Moon may create situations where it is difficult to access comfort, compassion, and the care you need. Saturn opposing the Moon brings up feelings of inadequacy. Reaching out for help may be challenging. You may have had a parent who was very withholding or emotionally unavailable. With this placement you need to give yourself permission to make mistakes, to learn from them, and to be open to constructive feedback.

- **Uranus** may speak to the inconsistencies of your early years, parents, and the traumas of your childhood. This aspect may create a desire to leave what feels stable and change what is familiar, as well as make it hard to build and maintain connections. You may have experienced a parent or caregiver as exciting, erratic, extreme, and experimental in ways that compromised your security.

- **Neptune** may create anxiety due to a lack of grounding in your life. You may find it hard to be emotionally consistent. You may be vulnerable to being fooled by others and have a hard time reading the intentions of those who wish to use or take advantage of you. You may have experienced a parent or caregiver as emotionally draining, or unable to hold their own boundaries, service their own needs, or show up for you with consistency. Being discerningly attentive to, instead of duped by, the displays of need around you will be important for developing your emotional maturity.

- **Pluto** may desire to control emotions, so much so that it is difficult to feel safe enough to be vulnerable, relaxed, and open with others. The opposite can also be true, and you may feel controlled, or overtaken by the whims, desires, and demands of others. You may need significant time processing emotions before you understand them; if not they can erupt like a volcano. A parent or caregiver may have had a personality that was overwhelming, controlling, intense, or draining to your system. In order to separate from them you may have had to go through a process of complete transformation and reinvention.

Mergers

CONJUNCTIONS

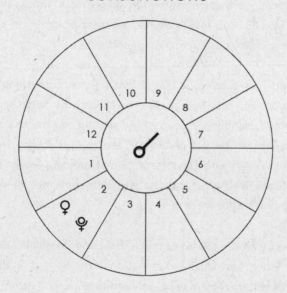

Since the Moon is so impressionable, the nature of any planet that is in the same sign as it can influence the style of the Moon greatly.

Your Moon conjunct . . .

- **Sun** brings the two lights of the chart together, signifying that the life's purpose and the way it gets lived out are done in the same style. When the Sun and Moon are together, it speaks to being born either at the end or the beginning of a lunar cycle, depending on the degrees of both.

- **Mercury** merges the need for comfort with communication. You may process feelings verbally, find comfort through communications that create bonds, or seek out those who think like you do. You may have had a parent or caregiver who was exceptionally chatty, witty, or good at sales.

- **Venus** is an auspicious aspect that signifies something of ease for you. You may be able to create bonds by being approachable and friendly, or beautiful and alluring, to others. Venus can always offer the gift of beauty, and that privilege can sometimes bring material comforts. Sometimes this aspect signifies someone with a parent who was attractive, people-pleasing, graceful, and/or artistic.

- **Mars** by nature causes us to overheat and, when placed next to the Moon, can cause inflammation in the body or in the emotional system. You may have a hard time cooling down, slowing down, and creating or sustaining bonds. A parent might have had no regard for your boundaries, much like the square or opposition from the Moon to Mars. You can be emotionally defensive and defended, and you need to learn how to find safety in yourself so that you can respect the boundaries of your body, your life, and others.

- **Jupiter** is extreme in its needs: it requires a lot, wants to give a lot, and desires to create ever more connection. Jupiter is generous, generative, and abundant, making this is a very auspicious signature, if not sometimes overwhelming. A parent may have had a larger-than-life persona that encouraged you to take up space or that dominated your environment, leaving little room for you.

- **Saturn** is going to be one of the more difficult conjunctions as the Moon and Saturn are so different. The Moon wants bonding, protections, safety, and nourishment, and Saturn is austere, creates boundaries and structures, and rejects what it is offered. Saturn tends to trick the Moon into feeling unworthy of sustenance. You may need to learn how to develop strong boundaries that allow for love and connection. You may have had a parent or caregiver who was remote, unavailable, successful, depressive, excessively productive, or felt like an oppressive force in your life.

- **Uranus** can have erratic relationships, often bouncing between needing comfort and needing space. People with this placement often come from a fragmented or eccentric family or may need to break from family tradition by creating their own. The individual may also need to create a home and family in a unique or different way. You may have experienced a parent or caregiver who was in circumstances that forced them to be erratic in their ability to show up for you. They may have been a very different kind of caregiver, or you may have not had enough consistent nurturing to ever feel satiated, emotionally or otherwise. Learning to give yourself what you need, every day, will go a long way toward your healing.

- **Neptune** merges with others creating a wealth of sensitivity, empathy, and compassion. However, you may have a hard time maintaining boundaries and need to learn how to differentiate yourself from others. You may have felt that a parent or caregiver didn't see you as a separate person and needed you to take care of them, especially if addiction or illness was a part of the relationship.

- **Pluto** creates an intense emotional life. You merge with others in powerful ways that can be exhausting or all-consuming. You might have obsessive feelings or have a parent or caregiver who did. You are most likely someone whom others are always coming to with their problems. You have an emotionally charismatic, even a little scary, air about you, and you exude power, affecting others in deep and perhaps unconscious ways. Your parent or caregiver may have had experiences where they felt consumed by a situation or another person, and as a result, you may not have felt seen or cared for. Your parent may have tried to overtake your personal boundaries, energy, and space, or that may have been their experience of their own life. Personal power and the use of it become looming themes in these dynamics.

Reflection Questions

- Which planets are helping your Moon? Do you feel their good graces? Do you ever downplay these gifts or take them for granted? How can you support yourself in making the most of this ease in your chart to live out your full potential?

- Which planets are impeding or challenging your Moon? Is it validating to learn this about your chart? How can you support yourself in understanding these challenges as growth edges, not immovable obstacles?

- What has been validated about your physical and emotional needs?

- How can you support yourself in making sure that you are nourished in the ways you need to be?

- What has been validated about the nature of your relationship to a parent? Does this validation give you permission to heal? Does it give you reason to give thanks for a particular parental relationship or to move on from the painful memory of one?

- After finishing this section, take care of yourself. Give yourself nourishment. Be kind to your body for the rest of the day. Remember that it is the physical manifestation of your soul's purpose and respect it accordingly.

V

YOUR ASCENDANT AND ITS RULER

*Your Motivation for Life and the
Steersperson of Your Ship*

Your Ascendant is the exact degree of the zodiac that was rising up over the eastern horizon at the moment you took your first breath. Because of this, your Ascendant is incredibly personal to you—the most personal point in your chart. The degree of the zodiac on the eastern horizon changes every few minutes, so the more exact you can get about your time of birth, the more personal the information you can glean from your Ascendant.

The Ascendant point is always in a sign, which is also referred to as your "rising sign." For example, if your Ascendant is in Sagittarius, you have Sagittarius rising. The nature of the sign that was on the eastern horizon as you entered the world symbolizes your motivation for being here. It tells us what gets you going, gets you out of bed, and sets you on the quest of life.

As Demetra George teaches in her book, *Astrology and the Authentic Self*, the Ascendant speaks to what we want to be known for. Fire rising signs—Leo, Aries, and Sagittarius—are motivated to, and want to be known for, taking action. Earth rising signs—Capricorn, Taurus, and Virgo—are motivated to, and want to be known for, building in a practical and steadfast way. Air rising signs—Libra, Aquarius, and Gemini—are motivated to, and want to be known for, their ability to communicate and exchange ideas. Water rising signs—Cancer, Scorpio, and Pisces—are motivated to, and want to be known for, creating and sustaining emotional bonds.

Because each sign is ruled by a planet, so is your Ascendant. The planet that rules your Ascendant is called the Ascendant ruler. It tells you what direction your life must take. It is, as Robert Schmidt described it, the "steersman" of the ship of your life. For example, if your Ascendant is in Aries, then the ruler of your Ascendant is Mars, because Aries is ruled by Mars. In other words, Mars is the steersperson of your ship.

The Rulers of Each Sign

- Aries ♈ is ruled by Mars ♂

- Taurus ♉ is ruled by Venus ♀

- Gemini ♊ is ruled by Mercury ☿

- Cancer ♋ is ruled by the Moon ☾

- Leo ♌ is ruled by the Sun ☉

- Virgo ♍ is ruled by Mercury ☿

- Libra ♎ is ruled by Venus ♀

- Scorpio ♏ is ruled by Mars ♂

- Sagittarius ♐ is ruled by Jupiter ♃

- Capricorn ♑ is ruled by Saturn ♄

- Aquarius ♒ is ruled by Saturn ♄

- Pisces ♓ is ruled by Jupiter ♃

To understand your Ascendant and how it shapes your motivation for life, it is helpful to explore the following four features:

1. What is your motivation for life? (What sign is your Ascendant?)

2. Who is influencing your motivation for life? (Do you have any planets in the same sign as your Ascendant?)

3. Who is steering the ship of your life? (What planet rules your Ascendant?)

4. What area of your life are you being steered toward? (What house is your Ascendant ruler in?)

Knowing what motivates us is half the battle to being happy. If we know that part of our particular motivation is to express and acknowledge deep emotional states of being, why would we waste another moment chastising ourselves for being sensitive? If we know that we are motivated in part by taking courageous action, why would we forsake our true nature by trying to be demure, aloof, or conservatively rule-abiding?

Radical self-acceptance means understanding that we were made exactly as we were meant to be. There is no part of us without a purpose. There is no excess in how we are put together. There was no mistake made here.

As you learn about the sign of your Ascendant, your Ascendant ruler, and the house your Ascendant ruler is in, notice what comes up for you and which parts of yourself you automatically judge, which you accept, and which you wish you were not.

Key Points to Remember about Your Ascendant and Ascendant Ruler

- The Ascendant is the exact point in the sky that was on the eastern horizon at the moment you took your first breath. It is determined by your time, date, and location of birth.

- The Ascendant is a point. The sign that your Ascendant is in is called your rising sign.

- Your Ascendant is your motivation for living and what you wish to be known for.

- Your Ascendant ruler is the planet that rules your Ascendant and rising sign.

- That planet is the steersperson of the ship of your life.

- The house that your Ascendant ruler is in tells you what area of life you are being steered toward.

CHECK IN WITH YOUR CHART

FINDING YOUR ASCENDANT

Look for this glyph ⬆ *in your chart.*
This is your Ascendant.

The Ascendant is always in the 1st House, the slice of pie on the left-hand side of your chart with the number 1 in it. The sign that it is in is your rising sign.

What is the sign of your Ascendant?

My Ascendant is in the sign of _____.

The planets in the same sign as my Ascendant are _____.
(*Remember that you may not have any.*)

Which planet rules your Ascendant?

The ruler of my Ascendant is _____.

The ruler of my Ascendant is in the sign of _____.

The ruler of my Ascendant is in the _____ **house of** _____.

SIGN OF YOUR ASCENDANT
WHAT IS YOUR MOTIVATION FOR LIFE?

What Sign Is Your Ascendant?

The sign of your Ascendant tells you the style with which you will find your way through this earthly experience. When we look to Frida Kahlo and Dr. Maya Angelou to see how their Ascendant informed their motivations in life, we get a glimpse as to what inspired them to become artists and activists. Both Kahlo and Angelou were born with Leo rising, which means their motivation was to self-express, to perform their inner experience to the world, and to enter into life in a dramatic, captivating manner that would draw attention to what they did. Leo is a fixed fire sign that has an intensity, strength, and power to it. Kahlo embodied this in her hundreds of self-portraits. Dr. Angelou, similarly motivated to creatively self-express, did so through her poetry, novels, essays, dance, television, movies, music, and scholarly work, which were recognized with numerous awards.

 Now it is time to choose your own adventure. Please skip ahead to the sign of your Ascendant, your rising sign.

ARIES RISING

♈ ☨

If your Ascendant is in Aries, you'll want to be known for your ability to launch into action. With great courage and little consideration for consequences, your Aries Ascendant needs the experience that only risk can reward you with. As a cardinal fire sign, Aries Ascendants need to headbutt their way into life. Much like impact helps the skeletal system to build bone density, crashing into things every now and again can build a kind of resilience that your Aries Ascendant will appreciate.

Aries rules the head and face. Having your Ascendant in this sign may make this area of your body prominent, prone to issues, or sensitive to touch. Just as your mascot, the ram, is in need of a worthy opponent, so are you. Though others might read your style as aggressive, your way of being in the world is straightforward. Be it in love, work, or leisure, your Aries Ascendant needs a little edge to stay interested.

Aries, ruled by Mars, will make you want to prove yourself through engaging in stressful, courageous acts that test your ability to struggle and emerge triumphant. You'll most likely be known for being an independent and assertive force of nature that will persevere or make whomever gets in your way suffer for doing so. This part of you needs you to apply your energy, otherwise it will backfire. When distorted, your Aries Ascendant can act like a match to the world's steady stream of gasoline.

👁 *Affirmations*

- I trust the intuitive responses I have to life.

- Every time I risk my reputation to follow my truth, I feel fortified.

📝 *Reflection Questions*

- What about this description of Aries resonates with you? What about this description motivates you?

- Where in your life do you regularly take actions that other people consider courageous?

- What do you tend to get competitive about? When does your competitiveness help you better yourself? When does it contribute to painful separations in your life?

TAURUS RISING

If your Ascendant is in the fixed earth sign of Taurus, you'll want to be known for your ability to stabilize available resources in order to make something beautiful and long-lasting out of them. Your Taurus Ascendant knows how to bring beauty into form. Ruled by Venus, planet of love, relationship, connection, pleasure, and people-pleasing, Taurus knows how to build a love nest that lasts. Ruling the neck, throat, and shoulders, your Taurus Ascendant may want these areas especially adorned with kisses, intoxicating elixirs, or bedazzling jewels.

Taurus's fixed nature makes you known for your stubbornness but also your ability to ground and manifest the potential that passes others by. Your Taurus Ascendant will remind you and others how to enjoy the simple pleasures of life. The sway of a tree branch. The sway of a hip. The sway of a sweetheart.

Your Taurus Ascendant naturally gathers others around you as you provide generous amounts of grounding nourishment. Taurus is generative, and the more you feel aligned with your own generativity, the more at home you are. Taurus is here to produce what it can from the land that is its life, cultivating good conditions for future growth over many seasons.

When distorted, your Ascendant can trick you into thinking it is safer to try and control, possess, or force life in a certain direction. Taurus is slow to anger, but once you've been pushed to your brink, your raging bull is hard to rein in.

👁 Affirmations

- I'm motivated to develop what feels generative, abundant, and stable.

- My persistence carries me to each and every finish line meant for me.

📝 Reflection Questions

- What about this description of Taurus resonates with you? What about this description motivates you?

- What do you tend to spend your life building, working toward, or solidifying?

- When does wanting and needing comfort, security, or pleasure impede your ability to experience new things?

GEMINI RISING

♊ ☼

Gemini is a trickster, mischief-maker, magician, salesperson, reporter, and gatherer and giver of information. Gemini could sell a broken wand to a wizard if it wanted to.

Having your Ascendant in this mutable air sign means that you'll want to be known for your ability to run relay races around any other news source. One of your great inspirations is to exchange facts, fictions, tidbits, and tantalizing morsels of meaning that you have been able to curate. Gemini has a story to tell everyone it meets.

Ever inquisitive, you are motivated by the search for intellectual stimulation and social connection. Your Gemini Ascendant will always try to see the situation from both sides, wanting to be not only comfortable with but inviting of contradictions, duality, and paradox. Charismatic to no end, your powers of persuasion will have you fluttering around the impermeable until you find a sliver of a crack to slip through.

Your Gemini Ascendant may be known for raising more questions than answers. Stasis is never the point. Forever in motion, the sign symbolized by the twins is happier when in dialogue than when in cemented certainty.

Gemini rules the arms and hands, as well as the lungs, as every good communicator needs the wind to carry forth its message. Gemini's ruling planet is Mercury, who retrogrades three to four times a year, journeying into the underworld. Changing directions. Needing to rethink things. Reviewing its options. Transforming through the process of mental purification. You might find yourself mimicking the journey of your ruling planet. When distorted, your Ascendant can appear inconsistent and ungrounded, causing others to doubt your intentions.

👁 *Affirmations*

- I am hardwired to exchange what I have with those around me.

- I am as reflective as I am inquisitive.

📝 *Reflection Questions*

- What about this description of Gemini resonates with you? What about this description motivates you?

- Are you known for your ability to communicate with others? What inspires you about gathering information and dispersing it in your own way?

- How does curiosity drive your daily life?

CANCER RISING

♋ ♎

Feeling is Cancer's forte. Cancer initiates us into our need to connect. To release the tears stuck in our ducts. To address our most neglected selves. Cancer creates security and safety through emotional bonds that feel or are familial.

If your Ascendant is in this cardinal water sign, you will be known for your ability to care for your cohorts, friends, and family members, initiating them into the realms of the heart.

Creating connection through intuiting and meeting the needs of others, your Cancer Ascendant will remember how your loved ones take their tea, how they feel about their parents, and what kind of color their eyes are when they're not happy. Cancer loves to feed and be fed, ruling the stomach and breasts.

Cancer holds memory. History. Ancestry. Tenacious beyond what might be healthy, your Cancer Ascendant will hold on past the expiration date of an experience.

Ruled by the Moon, your moods fluctuate. Luna is constantly blooming, releasing, and being reborn, revealing your need to be in a continuing cycle of death and rebirth. The Moon reminds us of how important it is not to get overly committed to one state or another.

When distorted, your energy can run moody, melancholy, and morbidly attached to the past. You may be overly sensitive and prone to taking things personally. The symbol for Cancer is the crab, whose hard shell can come off as defensive despite the most tender of underbellies.

👁 *Affirmations*

- I am motivated to feel and be felt.

- I give care where I know it is appreciated and desired.

📝 *Reflection Questions*

- What about this description of Cancer resonates with you? What about this description motivates you?

- Do your moods tend to impede your ability to be consistent in how you show up in the world? How do you manage this?

Do you become overly defensive when you feel unexpectedly vulnerable? What helps you when this happens?

- Do you enter the world sussing out who needs to be taken care of? How do you feel when you've been helpful, nurturing, or loving to others? How do you manage your expectations of others?

LEO RISING

♌ ☀

With no shame in shining, Leo knows that any performance is, at its core, a spiritual act. The actor gets up on stage and allows the human condition, in all its glory and its goriness, to come forth in service of the whole. We need a true reflection of our pain, beauty, and burdens. It's healing to witness someone else go through what we ourselves deal with. This is Leo's gift.

Ready to make the crowd roar with laughter, your Leo Ascendant, like its planetary ruler, the Sun, is born to be the center of the situation. This fixed fire sign has you famously expressing yourself and thus drawing attention your way. Others in your presence, knowingly or not, will become the audience to your performance. Your Leo Ascendant needs to be appreciated, loved, and adored for whatever it is that you are offering.

Leo rules the heart and spine. Your swagger stimulates the system. Raising heart rate. Increasing blood flow. Playful and spontaneous, your Leo Ascendant will be known for your love of drama and the power of a good entrance. Like the nobility its planetary ruler (the Sun) signifies, Leo is quite comfortable in a crown.

This sign distorted becomes obsessed with itself. Egomaniacal, domineering, and self-absorbed tendencies constellate in Leo's lair. The lion, ever prideful, can lash out when provoked. Exuding a powerful presence, you'll need to learn what stages your Leo Ascendant wants to set aglow.

👁 *Affirmations*

- I allow myself full self-expression.

- I am here to let my light shine while enjoying the brilliance of those around me.

📝 *Reflection Questions*

- What about this description of Leo resonates with you? What about this description motivates you?

- What do you generally receive attention for? Is it positive? Negative? Do you admonish yourself for needing a certain amount of recognition, love, applause, or appreciation?

- What do you most want to be known for? What do you most want to be celebrated for? Are you known for having a playful demeanor? Is that important to you? Are you known for being a diva? Is that important to you?

VIRGO RISING

♍ ♎

With your Ascendant in Virgo, the mutable earth sign, you'll be known for your ability to make the information you have access to useful. Practical. Applicable. Through the development of your skill, your Virgo Ascendant will be happiest when working on something meaningful to you. Never finished perfecting whatever you are fixated on in the moment, your ability to pinpoint what doesn't work is mind-boggling to the rest of the world.

Virgo is exacting, critical, deeply introspective, intrigued with intelligent systems—especially ones that are healing, efficient, and naturally occurring. Your Ascendant is motivated to analyze, digest, and integrate the information that you acquire. Virgo is always in the process of putting things together and removing what isn't needed. As such, it rules the small intestines, diaphragm, spleen, and bowels. This makes you adept at cleansing the physical, emotional, and intellectual system. A natural healer, health care provider, or medical professional, your Ascendant is motivated to find the root of the issue to bring healing to the whole.

Virgo's symbol is the virgin, usually with a sheaf of wheat and bird to depict the double-bodied nature of this mutable sign. In the ancient world, the term *virgin* referred to those who belonged to themselves, not someone who had never had sex. Dedicated to discovering one's own nature through disciplined devotion, the Virgin uses the practice of self-regeneration as a way to connect spiritually. This can lend you a style that others read as closed off, unapproachable, or aloof when really you are just internally busy.

What others may not understand is that Virgo is excruciatingly sensitive. Beneath the ability to critique is a deep desire to align. Virgo purifies and, in love, Virgo needs a partner who is willing to constantly process the material of the moment.

When Virgo is distorted, your exacting ways are turned inward. Your Virgo can find fault with so much that you either convince yourself you have nothing to give or that no one and nothing is good enough to pursue. You'll need to develop a keen ability to intercept your own self-sabotage, self-loathing, or self-scrutiny and instead turn that energy toward work in service of something greater.

👁 Affirmations

- I am dedicated to serving what is sacred to me.

- I am patient when others are still learning what I already know.

📝 Reflection Questions

- What about this description of Virgo resonates with you? What about this description motivates you?

- Are you known for being a hard worker? Is overworking yourself second nature to you? Do you tend to overdo what you are working on? Do you tend to overanalyze things, and does that impede your ability to do the work you need to? Do you ever use work as a way to avoid intimacy, pleasure, or living some aspect of your life?

- What do you tend to be overly critical about with yourself? What do you tend to get overly critical about with others? How does this impede intimacy in your life?

LIBRA RISING

♎ ☍

Your Libra Ascendant is motivated to initiate relationships. This cardinal air sign has an uncanny ability to connect with anyone, anywhere, and at any time if it wants to. Even if you are extremely introverted, your Libra Ascendant will lean toward being sociable, pleasant to be around, and understanding of others' ups and downs.

Ruled by Venus, Libra reaches out in ways that want to put others at ease. Your Libra Ascendant can most likely get others to do things for you without them even being aware. Mere suggestion is potent when delivered by someone who is so disarmingly likable.

Beauty and being inspired by art, design, and the delicate nature of harmony are high on your list of valuable assets. In most situations, you'll be motivated to create peace and avoid unnecessary discord.

Libra's symbol is the scales, and as such, you may feel obligated to balance out whatever situation you find yourself in. Libra rules the kidneys, the organs that balance the electrolytes in our system. What is out of balance can become a point of obsession. Plagued with the thought of making the wrong decision, your Libra Ascendant may well weigh a choice until the cows come home.

Libra intuitively seeks out ways in which it can make up for the lack in any situation. Flustered at the thought of anyone being upset, your Libra Ascendant may have you burdened with the false notion that it's your job is to make sure that people are pleased. The endless pursuit of making sure everyone is content is a losing game.

Distraught by injustice, your Libra Ascendant will need to know every side of a situation. You may have a hard time drawing hard lines and you'll have to be mindful of your ability to shop out your decision-making power. Never wanting to be seen as the cause of harm or disruption, your Libra Ascendant may try to position you as blameless, but there is no such thing. In order to be in the ring of life, you'll have to be able to take a position. Otherwise, you end up nowhere.

Distorted, Libra can come off as insincere, fixated on aesthetic beauty, and unable to be direct. To counter this, you'll most likely need to work on cultivating inner balance and self-love.

👁 Affirmations

- I am here to experience what balance might be like in any given moment.

- When pursuing justice, I put myself in the equation.

📝 Reflection Questions

- What about this description of Libra resonates with you? What about this description motivates you?

- Is it difficult for you to do things that you feel might disappoint others? Are you constantly weighing what you need to do against what others want you to do or want from you?

THE THIRD KEY: YOUR ASCENDANT AND ITS RULER // 175

- Are you driven to create justice, beauty, or connection between the people you love?

- When you see or experience injustice, on any level, what happens to your body, mind, and heart?

SCORPIO RISING

Scorpio, the fixed water sign, is famous for its ability to penetrate even the strongest of surfaces, reaching far below the obvious into the unknown territory of a situation. Ruled by Mars, the warrior, the spear, the weapon, having a Scorpio Ascendant means that you'll be motivated to get to the truth no matter what is in your way.

Most likely, you'll be known for being strategic. Patient. Perceptive. Powerful. Able to wait until what you want makes its way to you. Your reserves of emotional strength are undeniable; they have to be if you are to carry out your mission. Immovable once you have made up your mind, your Scorpio Ascendant gives you the strength to never doubt your decision. Powerful enough to demolish anything that gets in its way, Scorpio energy is relentless in its efforts. No trial is too great. Its resilience is unmatched. Its intensity unwavering. This is, quite possibly, why you don't make decisions impulsively. Once on course, good luck to anyone who tries to divert you. Stubborn doesn't even begin to explain your staying power.

Ruling the organs of reproduction and elimination, Scorpio isn't fazed by the kink of any imagination. Down to explore the possibilities of power and playfulness, Scorpio has a reputation for its sexual magnetism. But that kind of stereotyping generally misses the mark. Scorpio often acts like a portal of transformation for others. Because it is comfortable with discomfort, Scorpio isn't afraid of the process of change. This intensity is alluring and alarming to others. Whether or not Scorpio is aiming to be, it makes a strong impression if nothing else.

Distorted, your Ascendant is capable of destructive and obsessive self-sabotage. You can turn your back on what you need most to prove a point. Unforgiving, Scorpio distorted would rather survive the harshest of conditions than give in to its opponent. To prove a point, you may notice that you aren't afraid to suffer—perhaps feeling too comfortable doing so. Quite often, Scorpio becomes the repository for all that we fear, but really it is this energy that helps us challenge, work through, and ultimately overcome those fears.

👁 Affirmations

- I direct my energy toward the people and places that appreciate its power and impact.

- I respect my strength by allowing myself to also be vulnerable.

📝 Reflection Questions

- What about this description of Scorpio resonates with you? What about this description motivates you?

- Do people tell you that you intimidated them when you first met? Do you have a mysterious persona that precedes you?

- Are you constantly looking for the ulterior motive of a person or situation?

- Do people often have emotional or cathartic experiences around you that they have a hard time understanding or that are profound for them?

SAGITTARIUS RISING

♐ ⛢

Sagittarius is the mutable fire sign that knows how to inject its goodwill into the world, no matter the circumstance. Ruled by the gas giant, Jupiter, Sagittarius knows not of understatement. On even the smallest of endeavors, with a Sagittarius Ascendant you will bring your full being, unbridled enthusiasm, and levity to the densest of dealings. Not known for its precision, your Sagittarius Ascendant will often have you setting off in the direction of your inspired desire rather than checking the map for specific directions.

But you'll get there.

With seemingly unending energy, this fire sign motivates you to roam, wander, and wonder about what is over the next horizon. A double-bodied sign, the centaur is half-human, half-horse. Half-tamed, half-wild, you lead with as much insight as you do impulse.

Generous and swift with both criticism and praise, you'll often end up in hot water for having said the thing no one else would. Swept up in the fever of your intuitive channeling, your Sagittarius Ascendant will have you famous for tearing through any and all filter placed on you.

As a child of the benevolent Jupiter, your Ascendant encourages you to leap into the unknown, assuming you will land fortunately. And usually that is true. It takes faith to have faith, and you have much to spare.

Ruling the legs and thighs, Sagittarius's energy would rather gallop than plod along, making the consequences you come up against abrupt but quickly over.

When Sagittarius energy is distorted, it creates an insatiable gluttony. Gloating about the glory days, the gambler risks what it doesn't have to play with. A greed for the next great high can consume you. To rectify this, you as the archer must aim your arrow at the truth and dedicate your whole being to boldly following its soaring release.

👁 Affirmations

- I am free to choose how I engage with my life.

- I always know when to go, when to stay, and when to investigate further, and I honor the intuitive wisdom that guides me.

📝 Reflection Questions

- What about this description of Sagittarius resonates with you? What about this description motivates you?

- Are you someone who brings optimism, opportunity, luck, and a generosity of spirit into your interactions with others?

- Are you known for overdoing things? Are you known for being able to do things that others see as impossible? Are you prone to biting off a little more than you can chew? How do you manage when you do?

CAPRICORN RISING

♑ ⛎

With a Capricorn Ascendant, you will be known for your ability to put to use whatever is at your disposal. Your mascot is the mystical sea-goat: the goat scales incredible heights along impossible impasses, while the fish possesses the dexterity to accomplish any task. You are motivated to perform phenomenal feats and incredible accomplishments over long stretches of time.

Capricorn's sharp sense of irony allows you to accept life on life's terms. Unfazed by the latest craze, your Capricorn Ascendant can appear as a grumpy, gray-haired wise one to the world. Adolescence is an uncomfortable condition for Capricorn. This Saturn-ruled sign does much better with age. Youth has many an enviable quality, but time is a teacher that has no competition.

Capricorn is concerned with the kind of rigorous training that demands lifelong learning and, with this Ascendant, you'll be known for your ability to age well. You are motivated to go after the pearls of wisdom that never fade in their luster. Your ability to focus on a goal and attain it is outdone by no one. Capricorn doesn't need comfortable conditions to thrive. You don't need special treatment, though you're never one to turn down an accolade, certificate, or societal recognition of effort.

Sustained by an inner fire, your Ascendant wants you to realize your goals with a mixture of deep contemplation and an unwavering drive to get things done. The fish-tail donned by the sea-goat points to the emotional depths to which your rising sign will have you travel. Oceans symbolize ancient realms of knowledge. Known for your emotional self-containment, you'll generally need to explore your own vulnerabilities in solitude. Ruling the bones and skin, your Capricorn Ascendant thrives when knowing the rules, boundaries, and shapes of a relationship.

When distorted, Capricorn is master of self-restriction, self-denial, self-rejection, and self-punishment. This is a sign that needs to remember how to let love, pleasure, and kindness in, especially when you feel that you have failed at a task.

👁 Affirmations

- I am here to accomplish great tasks and experience great love and affection.

- I honor the time it takes to master what is most meaningful to me.

📝 Reflection Questions

- What about this description of Capricorn resonates with you? What about this description motivates you?

- Are you known as someone who is mature and responsible? When has this felt like a burden or been taken advantage of? When has it helped you?

- Do you often restrain yourself, feel it necessary to withhold pleasure from yourself, or go without what others would deem essential? What does this help you achieve, and what does it hinder you from experiencing?

AQUARIUS RISING

♒ ♌

Aquarius isn't convinced by sentiment. It isn't held captive by nostalgia. It isn't fooled by flattery. A fixed air sign, Aquarius has remarkable intellectual gifts. With this sign as your Ascendant, you'll be known for your ability to understand the systems you live within and to innovate them for the betterment of all involved.

With this as the sign of your Ascendant, you won't be satisfied to follow the herd. You define yourself by thinking for yourself. Unafraid to stand apart from the group or be ostracized for your ideas, your Aquarius Ascendant is socially conscious, but not at all interested in people-pleasing.

Since you don't reach conclusions lightly, you aren't easily swayed. Ruled by Saturn, Aquarius is able to separate fact from fiction. Saturn-ruled signs have a deep respect for logic, boundaries, and systems. You might not adhere to them, but you will be thoroughly versed in the rules of the game.

Wanting to be known for your clarity, certainty, and thoughtful perspective, you'll need to demonstrate your fearlessness when witnessing the truth or telling it. The water bearer of the zodiac pours forth the libations that humanity thirsts for. Whether the world protests or not, your Aquarius Ascendant is sturdy enough to take any backlash offered without taking it personally.

The cleansing nature of Aquarius's waters are universal creative intelligence brought into being. Though not a water sign, Aquarius does rule the circulation of blood in the body, as well as the ankles. Since Saturn is its ruler, the circulation in the body can often be restricted, adding a literal and physical manifestation of this sign's notorious coolness.

Distorted, Aquarius is clinical in its perceptions. Logic divorced from the wisdom of the heart can only contain partial truths. Aloof and emotionally distant, Aquarius can lock itself away in an ivory tower of intellectual protection, but emotional intelligence should not be underestimated. Aquarius must learn that emotions have their own brilliance, leading us to the truth of a situation that logic alone cannot find.

ૐ Affirmations

- I honor my need to be known for my intellect.

- Vulnerability has its own wisdom.

✎ Reflection Questions

- What about this description of Aquarius resonates with you? What about this description motivates you?

- Are you known for your intellectual clarity? How does this serve you? How does it hinder you?

- Do you enter the world wanting to understand the systems that we live in, how to work within them, and how to subvert, reform, or innovate them?

PISCES RISING

♓ ♎

Perhaps the most mutable of signs, the waters of Pisces cannot be contained. Herding fish swimming in opposite directions should not be attempted by those who wish to use their energy wisely. Anyone who tries to control you will be met with an inconspicuous master of self-defense. Your Pisces Ascendant is motivated to experience life, not to control or be controlled by it.

A double-bodied water sign, your Pisces Ascendant is motivated to move in every direction, gathering influences from multiple sources and dispersing your energy in various ways. Often ending up feeling spent, one of your greatest challenges will be learning how to conserve your life force and direct it toward your aim.

Pisces permeates, seeps, spreads, and evaporates without a trace. You will most likely be known for your ability to erode even the most stoic and stern of people, places, and boundaries. Like waves on the rocks, the impact of your Pisces Ascendant on others is felt as unending compassion, kindness, and empathy— the kind that wears down those who refuse you for no good reason. A natural nurse, healer, and physician, your knowledge of pain and the cure (generally kindness) is a balm with endless applications. As the artist or poet, your Pisces Ascendant knows how to infuse any medium with its creativity, imagination, and emotional relatability.

Ruled by Jupiter, Pisces is fertile and generative. As a water sign, Pisces is constantly intuiting the emotional experiences of others, and because it has access to the cures, it feels compelled to address the wounds of those who aren't ready to heal.

When distorted, your Pisces Ascendant may garner you the reputation of being a martyr, without boundaries, structure, or a direction. Charming your way out of responsibilities, your Pisces Ascendant's likability can work against your need to develop discipline. Ruling the feet, Pisces will need to find a way to ground themselves in the world and not give in to the temptation to swim away.

👁 Affirmations

- I go with the flow while honoring my needs.

- As I witness you, I am better able to witness myself.

📝 Reflection Questions

- What about this description of Pisces resonates with you? What about this description motivates you?

- Do you find ways to escape from situations that are uncomfortable, boring, or overwhelming for you? How does this help you? How does it hinder you?

- Do you have the ability or propensity for shape-shifting, depending on the situation that you are in? Do you tend to lose yourself in others? Are you overly susceptible to absorbing the emotions, moods, and issues of those around you?

PLANETS IN THE SAME SIGN AS YOUR ASCENDANT

WHO IS INFLUENCING YOUR MOTIVATION FOR LIFE?

In addition to understanding the meaning and implications of your rising sign, understanding the nature of any planets that are present in your 1st House is also important when trying to understand your motivation for living, your expression of that motivation, and what you want to be known for. This is because the Ascendant is in—and is synonymous with—the 1st House.

The 1st House is the only house in the chart solely dedicated to you. It is the house of body, self, appearance, and identity; therefore any planet in the 1st House will be woven into your personality in a very intimate and obvious way.

In general, planets in the 1st House will have extra strength and will have a major impact on how you express yourself. Not everyone has planets in their 1st House. If there are no planets in your 1st House, fear not. It isn't rare or unusual to have houses that are empty of planets. In fact, it's impossible to have a planet in every house. If you do have planets in the 1st House, remember that they have an enormous impact on your identity, appearance, mannerisms, and physical experience.

For example, if you have a fun-loving, faith-driven, optimistic Sagittarius rising, and you also have a stern and stately Saturn in Sagittarius in the 1st House, this changes the nature of how you'll express that Sagittarius rising. No longer unleashed upon the world in its raw and extreme state, your Sagittarius rising now has to pass through the filter of Saturn, so to speak. With this combination, you still want to be known as someone who is inspired and action-oriented (Sagittarius), but also as someone who is disciplined, responsible, and autonomous (Saturn). Saturn in the 1st House is reserved. Sagittarius rising is anything but. Therefore Saturn in Sagittarius in the 1st House needs to find a way to inspire others, demonstrate its ability to act on its intuition, and show up as someone who does so with great self-discipline.

Each planet in the 1st House will vie for control over how you express yourself. If you have multiple planets here, you may notice that you've got to juggle a great many paradoxes in your personality.

In general, any planet in the 1st House is going to be active in your lived experience. The closer in degree (especially within 3 degrees) to the Ascendant, the more active the planet will be in your life.

Astrological charts, just like the humans and situations that they represent, will be paradoxes. You might have a Libra rising with Mars in Libra in your 1st House. How do you keep the peace and initiate relationships (Libra rising) while being a self-directed warrior (Mars in the 1st House)?

This is the rub of being human.

Dr. Angelou had Neptune in the 1st House. Neptune is the planet of transcendence, escapism, idealism, and fantasy. Neptune in the 1st House can give the person who has this placement a certain otherworldly effect. Any planet in the 1st House is going to feature prominently in the person's life, wanting to be expressed through the vehicle of the self (1st House). In this case, Neptune influenced the way in which Dr. Angelou's Leo Ascendant expressed itself, adding an ethereal quality to her persona.

Because Neptune erodes boundaries that inhibit connection, we can consider how it may have helped Dr. Angelou's work and personality feel so resonant with so many. Her autobiographical novels are poignant, timeless, and full of depth and meaning, but were often criticized as not always being chronologically correct. Someone with Neptune in the 1st House may be more concerned with leaving the right impression, feeling, and vision than being precise about dates, times, and details.

 Now it is time to choose your own adventure. If you have any planets in the 1st House, please skip ahead to read about that planet. If there are no planets in your 1st House, go to the next section to read about the planet that rules your Ascendant.

WHO IS INFLUENCING YOUR MOTIVATION FOR LIFE?

Do You Have Any Planets in the Same Sign as Your Ascendant?

SUN IN THE 1ST HOUSE

The Sun in the 1st House will give your personality extra vibrancy and an ability to shine. You need to live out your life's purpose through being yourself and mastering your self-expression. Having the Sun here means that you were born around sunrise, that you have the same Sun sign as you do rising sign, and that you carry forth the energy of daybreak in your personality.

Reflection Questions

- Do you feel especially motivated toward self-expression? How has this manifested in your life? How would you like it to?

- Do you receive feedback that you have a strong persona or personality? How does this make you feel?

- Are you very energetic or physically strong? What does this help you to accomplish?

MOON IN THE 1ST HOUSE

The Moon in the 1st House will give you an added sensitivity to life, a changeability, and possible moodiness. To embody the Moon is to always be in flux. Since the Moon is a reflective surface, you may have an ability to mirror others—an irresistible quality to possess most of the time. Everyone yearns to feel reflected, seen, and acknowledged. Having the Moon in the 1st House helps you to connect with others by way of reflecting them.

Reflection Questions

- Do you tend to be known as someone who is emotionally receptive, caring, sensitive, and changeable? What do these qualities help you to do in life? What do they make difficult at times?

- Do you notice that your moods impact your physical energy a lot? What helps you move through difficult feelings?

- Does the shape of your body or your style tend to fluctuate greatly? Can you appreciate these changes just like you can appreciate the different phases of the Moon?

MERCURY IN THE 1ST HOUSE

Mercury in the 1st House is not only well placed because it is in the 1st House, but it is doubly blessed because the 1st House is the place of its joy. Mercury in the 1st House will make communication and exchanges with others central to your identity.

Reflection Questions

- Are writing, communicating, teaching, learning, or the magical arts a big part of your identity or what you are known for? Which of these crafts are you particularly skilled at? When did you first come to understand that you were?

- Do you tend to consume a lot of information, have a strong mind, or possess the ability to communicate with great clarity? What do you do with this talent?

- Is your style changeable? Do people often not recognize you from one day to the next? What does your versatility open up access to?

VENUS IN THE 1ST HOUSE

Venus in the 1st House will promote a pleasing persona, one that focuses on attracting what it wants and needs through graciousness, beauty, and creativity. Venus's main job is to come together with others in a pleasing and harmonious way, so this becomes a part of your personality and its agenda. Venus in the 1st House is a blessing; the only potential curse is not being able to ask for what you need for fear of upsetting others.

 Reflection Questions

- Are you motivated to create connections, beauty, and love? How do you do so?

- Are you known for being approachable? What does this bring you? When does it tend to overwhelm your system? Is it hard for you to refuse people?

- Do people tend to like you without you doing much? Do you often attract attention, solicited or not? What does it impede in your life? What does it help?

MARS IN THE 1ST HOUSE

♂

With Mars in the 1st House, you will be known as someone who needs to fight, with or without a cause. This placement is a little easier for those who are encouraged to be brave, challenging, and action-oriented. Mars's positive attributes get a chance to thrive if you have been applauded for your independence. Courage reigns supreme if you have Mars in the 1st House. Mars is the warrior, and a respected warrior functions differently from one that is misunderstood or, worse, condemned for its fighting spirit. When Mars runs up against difficulty (e.g., in a difficult sign, or in a difficult aspect to Saturn), it finds conflict easily and resolution with greater challenge, making life a lesson in conflict resolution for you. Mars in the 1st House may also signify that you have some kind of inflammation in the body that needs to be tempered, cooled, and calmed.

Reflection Questions

- Are you known for taking risks? What does this reputation mean to you? What does life feel like when there are no appropriate risks to take?

- Are you more motivated the more action you take? What generally motivates you to take action?

- Are you drawn toward doing what others deem brave? Does this sometimes result in you being told that you are divisive or argumentative? What do you do with that feedback?

JUPITER IN THE 1ST HOUSE

♃

Jupiter in the 1st House will magnify your impact on the world. Jupiter is big. It makes itself known and in the 1st House will give you the same impact. It's a planet that creates more of whatever it touches. It can give you an unstoppable buoyancy or appetite for life when in the 1st House. This can give you a reputation for having a physical prominence, a bombastic laugh, a spirit of generosity, a spirituality, and an abundance or opulence that precedes you. Jupiter can be quite excessive and in the 1st House can create a desire for great quantities of whatever interests you.

Reflection Questions

- Are you known for your generosity? What do you find this brings you, teaches you, or opens up for you?

- Do you tend to bring an abundant sense of goodwill, creating your own luck wherever you go? Where did you learn this? What do you learn from doing so?

- Are you known for your knowledge or interest in healing, medicine, or wisdom traditions? What do you do with these talents?

- Are you driven to manifest abundance in the world? What kind of abundance? What makes you feel most abundant?

SATURN IN THE 1ST HOUSE

Saturn in the 1st House is tricky, as it means that you are asked to embody the planet of boundaries, discipline, and rejection. Saturn can certainly lend you professionalism, maturity, and a desire to develop yourself into something substantial, but can also lead you to dismiss what brings joy and abundance. Because the 1st House is the body, Saturn in the 1st House can slow you down, inhibit your movement or create a stiffness in the body. Responsibilities may feel more like a burden than a stepping-stone toward self-development (at least at first). Saturn in the 1st House can create a kind of austere, serious, remote, and cool style or tone to your personality or appearance. Here, Saturn wants to help you learn self-mastery, honoring age and the wisdom it brings.

Reflection Questions

- Do you tend to feel a constriction in your body or tension in your muscles? What helps you loosen up?

- Do you often tell people no? Do you feel like you have more than your share of responsibility or feel driven to set boundaries with others? In what ways does this become taxing or burdensome on your system?

- Are you motivated to become a master at what you do? How so? Do you work hard at developing your authority? What gets in your way when trying to do so?

The Modern Planets

Remember that Uranus, Neptune, and Pluto aren't rulers of signs in traditional astrology and therefore aren't in "good or bad" condition in any particular sign. They are extreme, but not as personally relevant. These planets move so slowly that generations of folks with the same rising sign will have these outer planets in the 1st House.

URANUS IN THE 1ST HOUSE
⛢

Uranus in the 1st House breeds unconventionality. It makes you a little more disruptive, eccentric, and electric. Uranus is an exciting influence, as you never know what it will change next. You need to find ways to direct your energy so that you can effectively disrupt what is out of date and in need of innovation.

Reflection Questions

- Are you motivated to disrupt systems that seem illogical to you? What usually happens as a result?

- Are you or have you ever been someone who is (or who is seen as) a rebel without a cause? What has this done to your self-perception?

- Are you able to change your life's direction, take big risks, or reinvent yourself out of the blue? Write about some of the times that you have done so. What have these changes been able to open up space for?

- Do others find this aspect of you exciting, invigorating, or agitating (especially if they need consistency and adherence to social norms)? How do you usually deal with the feedback?

NEPTUNE IN THE 1ST HOUSE

Neptune in your 1st House lends you the ability to connect to many people. This planet makes boundaries porous and can erode your own. It can imbue your personality with an incredible imagination and an ability to shape-shift and be many things to many people. With Neptune here, you can easily lose yourself in the fantasies others have of you. Often overwhelmed by the needs and emotions of others, Neptune in the 1st House can require that you learn how to enforce your personal boundaries. Neptune can lend a glamorous and transcendent nature to you, which can further others' fascination with you.

✍ Reflection Questions

- Are you known for your compassionate presence, your innate sense of what others are going through, and your ability to merge or mesh with whomever you are around? What about these attributes are helpful? What about them causes you difficulty?

- Does your versatility sometimes make it hard for you to know what you want, or has it at certain times in your life made it hard for you to know who you are? Describe a couple of instances.

- Is creativity, spirituality, and being of service to others grounding and centering to you? Where in your life are you doing this in a way that helps you feel reenergized?

PLUTO IN THE 1ST HOUSE

Pluto in the 1st House lends you a depth and personal intensity. Pluto can create obsessive personality traits that can be redirected toward in-depth study, investigation, and the facilitation of one's personal power for good. Pluto wants to plunge into the depths of life, and with Pluto in the 1st House, you may require activities that invoke many a transformative experience.

Reflection Questions

- Are you known as someone who is constantly reinventing yourself? What initiates these transformations?

- Are you known as a powerful person? How do you channel your power into creating positive change in the world?

- Are you someone whom others have a powerful, cathartic, and possibly healing experience around? Do you ever feel like folks stick around for as long as they need to be healed and then move on? Do you ever feel that others lean on you for strength instead of doing the hard work of developing their own? What have these experiences taught you in terms of taking care of yourself?

- Do you tend to attract influential people to you? Have you had many extreme experiences as a result? Write about a couple of them.

PLANET THAT RULES YOUR ASCENDANT
WHO IS STEERING THE SHIP OF YOUR LIFE?

What Planet Rules Your Ascendant?

If we want to know what kind of journey we must go on in order to feel like we are living our life's purpose, we need to know which planet rules our Ascendant. The planet that rules the sign of your Ascendant is the planet that steers your life's direction in one way or another.

Each planet has a specific job to do: the Sun self-expresses, the Moon reflects and emotes, Mercury communicates, Venus creates beauty and builds relationships, Mars defends and protects, Jupiter expands through optimism, and Saturn builds structures and erects boundaries.

If we want to know the nature, the energy, and the emphasis of the driving desire of our life, the planet that rules our Ascendant will tell us as much. If we want to know the challenges and gifts that lay along our path, this planet will point to what we cannot ignore.

Some of us have an Ascendant ruler—a steersperson—that is efficient, empowered, and capable of moving our life forward (like a planet in a sign, it does well in its domicile or exaltation). Some of us have a steersperson who is a little more challenged, leading us down many different avenues that are both diversions and important departures (like a planet in a sign it struggles in— its detriment or fall). Some of us have a steersperson who is in a sign that it is fairly neutral in (any sign that isn't its domicile, detriment, exaltation, or fall) and will operate in the nature of that sign.

In this chapter, I detail each planet in its domicile, detriment, exaltation, and fall. It's important to know the ruler of your Ascendant's tendencies. Does it get off track? Is it especially empowered and maybe a little extreme? Is it going to help you receive some notoriety for its specialty? Or is it going to function in the style of the sign it's in with little complication? Because the following guide is fairly thorough, you can also apply it to any other planet in your chart. For example, if you have Venus in Pisces, the sign of its exaltation, but it isn't the ruler of your Ascendant, you'll still benefit from the information given.

Both Dr. Maya Angelou and Frida Kahlo have Leo rising. The Sun rules both of their Ascendants. When the Sun (or Moon) is also the ruler of the Ascendant, the emphasis on that luminary is noteworthy. As we have learned, the significance of both the Sun and Moon shouldn't be underestimated, and when one of them is also ruler of the Ascendant, it's doing double duty. With the Sun ruling both of their Ascendants, we know that how they shined (the sign the Sun was in when they were born) was not only significant in terms of living out their purpose (the Sun) but also spoke to the direction in which their life was steered (the ruler of their Ascendant). Because the ruler of Dr. Angelou's Ascendant, the Sun, was in Aries (bold and daring), the sign of its exaltation, she was gifted with a steersperson that was able to do its job efficiently, even granting her fame and recognition. Kahlo's Sun was in a neutral sign, Cancer, so the Sun steered her life in a way that was emotive, caring, and sensitive. Because the Sun is neither strong nor hindered in Cancer, we look to other factors to determine how easy or challenging it was to live out her life's purpose, namely, the house that the ruler of the Ascendant is in and the aspects to it from other planets.

 Now it is time to choose your own adventure. Please skip ahead to the planet that rules your rising sign.

SUN AS RULER (LEO RISING)

If you have a Leo Ascendant, the Sun becomes its ruler. This gives you two planets to focus on (the Sun and Moon) instead of three (the Sun, Moon, and separate ruler of the Ascendant).

When the Sun is the ruler of your Ascendant, your life's direction is steered toward developing your sense of self and puts an added emphasis on the house that your Sun lives in and the area of life it is here to illuminate. With the Sun as the Ascendant ruler, the way in which you express yourself, demonstrate your courage, and exude self-confidence becomes central to your story and ability to live out your life's purpose. Whatever sign the Sun is in will reveal your style for doing what you do. For more information about the sign that your Sun is in, please reread the description of your Sun's sign.

📝 Reflection Questions

- With the Sun as ruler of your Ascendant, what do you notice about your energy when you spend time and resources developing your sense of self?

- How does the development of self positively impact, or intimately link to, your life's purpose?

- Where in your life do you most want to be able to shine?

- What are you better able to serve when you feel acknowledged, witnessed, or applauded?

MOON AS RULER (CANCER RISING)

If you have a Cancer Ascendant, the Moon becomes its ruler. In a way, this makes your job a little easier, as you have only two planets to focus on (the Sun and Moon) instead of three (the Sun, Moon, and separate ruler of the Ascendant).

When the Moon is the ruler of your Ascendant, your life's direction is steered toward being able to reflect, emote, care, build bonds, and find ways to embody the power of your life's purpose in all that you do. As the Moon reflects the brilliance of your soul's purpose (the Sun), it does so through little daily rituals, activities, and everyday accomplishments. Finding your way to manifest your potential in this world, a little bit at a time, honors the potency, impact, and power of your life's direction.

As ruler of your Ascendant, the Moon will steer your life toward connection, familial-type bonds, daily and spiritual rituals, and practices that help you regenerate your energy. The sign your Moon is in will reveal the specific style in which your life's purpose is lived out. For more information about the sign that your Moon is in, please reread the description of your Moon's sign.

📝 Reflection Questions

- Where in your life is emotional reflection an integral part of your success?

- What do you find others are generally asking you to reflect back to them?

- How do you feel when you are able to help others?

- How is your success tied to being able to work through your own emotions? How is your success tied to helping others witness and manage their own emotions? How do you help yourself and others be more connected to the body?

MERCURY AS RULER
(GEMINI RISING, VIRGO RISING)

When Mercury is the ruler of your Ascendant, your life's direction is steered toward being able to communicate, learn, distribute, facilitate, and deliver the information most important to you. The sign that Mercury is in will reveal the distinct style in which you do this.

You can honor Mercury by making sure that you have as many interesting things to learn as you do to teach. Mercury is a planet of duality; honor this by always taking in and giving out the information that you have acquired.

The sign Mercury is in in your chart will tell you the specific style in which to move toward your life's main aim. Remembering that not every planet has the same clarity, strength, or ability in each sign, you will want to know how well the planet that steers the ship of your life can do its job.

Below are explanations of Mercury through the signs. Please read the description of your Mercury and answer any of the questions that resonate with you.

At Home and at Ease: **Mercury in Gemini or Virgo**

If the ruler of your Ascendant is Mercury and it's in Gemini or Virgo, it has an easier time doing the job of steering your life, because Mercury is at home (in its domicile) in these two signs. Mercury's currency is knowledge. In Gemini and Virgo, Mercury has incredible strength and is in many cases extreme in its intellectual abilities and pursuits. This is a "good" thing, but it won't make life easy per se. It will, however, make your talent more obvious.

MERCURY IN GEMINI

In Gemini, its air-sign home, Mercury focuses on how best it can gather, interpret, and distribute knowledge. Reporting on the data that it has, this planet offers a stream of unfiltered information. Getting the message across with great speed is more important than sorting through what it is delivering. Mercury in Gemini is chatty. Able to give and receive information without getting too weighed down by the emotional impact of it. It is simply here to gather and disperse.

MERCURY IN VIRGO

In Virgo, its earth-sign home, Mercury analyzes, categorizes, and integrates information. Here, Mercury is both in its domicile and exalted (the only planet to be in its domicile and exaltation in the same sign). Obsessed with organizing and utilizing the information that it has, Mercury as ruler of Virgo cares more about correcting the information it gathers than amassing ever more of it (like it may in Gemini). Mercury in Virgo is thoughtful in its approach. Mindful. Critical. Exact. Analytical to the extreme. It is concerned with the digestion, assimilation, and integration of knowledge. It is concerned with the proper placement and categorization of what it gathers. It is precision personified.

Magic and Mayhem: **Mercury in Sagittarius or Pisces**

Mercury experiences difficulty in Sagittarius (its detriment) and Pisces (its fall), as both signs are more concerned with the big picture, not the individual strokes it takes to paint it. If Mercury is the ruler of your rising sign and is in Sagittarius or Pisces, don't despair! Do learn how you may sometimes get lost along your path. Remember that the challenges in your chart are the places in yourself that you most need to develop and pay attention to. Doing so often gives you the skills that help you make incredible strides.

MERCURY IN SAGITTARIUS

Mercury in Sagittarius is in its detriment, which means it has to function in a style that is foreign to it. While Sagittarius seeks the ultimate truth, it can miss many of the details, facts, and foundational knowledge that it needs. Mercury in Sagittarius loves to go on great adventures to distant and far-off lands, but does it have the time, energy, and resources to complete its task? Along the way, Mercury discovers all kinds of interesting ideas, but it can often overwhelm itself with the sheer volume of information it acquires. Sagittarius always goes big. Mercury in Sagittarius will spout facts at you all day long if you let it. It will take you on grand informational adventures. It will go farther than it needs to, but that often means that it ends up halfway around the world when it only needed to go down the block.

If your rising sign is Gemini or Virgo and your Mercury is in Sagittarius, it will be important for you to learn how to stay on track, completing the tasks at hand in ways that don't waste too many resources.

MERCURY IN PISCES

Mercury in Pisces is in its fall, meaning that it struggles to be known, appreciated, or valued for the job that the planet is supposed to do. Planets in their fall are much like people who have fallen into disrepute. Mercury in Pisces isn't going to necessarily be known for its clarity. Pisces tends toward the poetic. The nonlinear. The nonbinary. The impressionistic. The feelings. The ethereal. Here Mercury can struggle to collect facts, as they don't necessarily hold its interest. Something doesn't have to be true to be right to this placement. Pisces is a sign that lives in its own reality, creating worlds within worlds. Here, Mercury can struggle with keeping focus, but it will always find something interesting to swim away with. If Mercury is the ruler of your rising sign and it is in Pisces, you'll need to find ways to channel your creativity and corral your energy toward your aim. Pisces wants to go everywhere at once, and as the planet that steers the direction of your life, this can make it challenging to focus your energy and attention on one thing. You may need multiple directions to pursue, but be careful not to expend all your energy in distractions.

Mercury in All the Other Signs

Mercury in Aries (bold and explicit), Taurus (slow and steady), Cancer (sensitive and intuitive), Leo (dramatic and illuminating), Libra (fair and just), Scorpio (deep and psychologically penetrating), Capricorn (pragmatic and strategic), and Aquarius (logical and thorough) is fairly neutral. Mercury in any of these signs isn't particularly weak or strong. Mercury in any of these signs will, of course, relay and receive information based on the style of the sign it is in. For example, Mercury in Aries as ruler of your rising sign will direct your life in an independent style and have you speaking in daring ways.

📝 Reflection Questions

- What are you communicating about when you feel most alive, encouraged, or purposeful in your life?

- What has teaching, writing, or distributing information opened up for you in terms of your life's direction?

- What are you drawn to learn about? Do you give yourself permission to do so? Do you take your need for learning seriously?

- What are you proficient at selling? What does this help you accomplish?

- Is your Mercury in a strong, challenging, or neutral sign? How does the style of the sign your Mercury is in speak to the ways in which you go about pursuing your life's direction?

VENUS AS RULER (LIBRA RISING, TAURUS RISING)

If you have Taurus or Libra Ascendant, Venus is its ruler. When Venus is the ruler of your Ascendant, your life's direction is steered by the planet that seeks love, beauty, and pleasure. The sentiment of your Sun or Moon might be contrary to Venus's desires, but if the planet of love and connection steers the direction of your life, you'll have to find ways to oblige.

You honor Venus when you seek pleasure, beauty, and bonds. The sign Venus is in will tell you the specific style in which you pursue these things and ultimately feel fully expressed in your life. Like every planet, Venus does especially well in some signs, struggles in others, and is fairly neutral in the rest.

Below are explanations of Venus through the signs. Please read the description of your Venus and answer any of the questions that resonate with you.

Pleasure and Prosperity: **Venus in Taurus or Libra**

Venus in Taurus or Libra has the power of its assets at its disposal. Venus is at home (domicile) in Taurus and Libra and will tend to lend you an adeptness at connecting with others as a way of fulfilling your life's purpose. A strong Venus will also be able to bring different elements together to create a harmonious, comfortable, and enjoyable experience. Art, beauty, and adornment are second nature to Venus in these signs.

VENUS IN TAURUS

In Taurus, Venus as ruler of the Ascendant will be driven to grow gardens of generative abundance for friends, lovers, colleagues, and the world at large. Venus in Taurus captivates its loves with sensual pleasures that are undeniably satiating. With the ruler of the Ascendant in one of its own signs, the orientation of your life is clear and direct—to build through relationships, art, beauty, and pleasure. If Venus and its significations of pleasure, delight, and beauty aren't part of the way in which your life is pursued, there won't be much satisfaction in it. Like all planets in their own sign, Venus in Taurus tends to be extreme, as nothing impedes it. You can get comfortable in any amount of ease and will generally have a difficult time galvanizing yourself into action.

VENUS IN LIBRA

In Libra, Venus is the master of initiating relationships. With this placement, your life's direction is pursued by being a captivating social butterfly who has the ability to connect to even the gloomiest of souls. You know how to make everyone feel witnessed when you want to.

Relationships, art, beauty, love, connection, and the expression of creative and erotic energy can become the center of your world (usually unconsciously) and can tend to overwhelm other aspects of your life. Often we take for granted our strengths or allow others to do so. Venus in Libra is so social and so interested in what is pleasing that, as the ruler of the Ascendant, it may steer your life only toward what is easy.

Gift from Goddess: *Exalted Venus in Pisces*

In Pisces, Venus is exalted and will attract all manner of connections. This placement is strong, and as the ruler of the Ascendant, it grants your life's direction some prosperity, luck, or an ability to attract what you need when you need it, usually through relationships with others. Like all planets that are exalted, Venus in Pisces will garner some kind of recognition or fame for Venus-like attributes.

You may experience frenzy around you. Those with deep relationship wounds will often make you their savior, object of affection, or obsession. You may feel the need to give of what you have if you didn't have to work at attaining this gift in the first place. Feeling confused as to why you have this power, you may have a hard time setting boundaries in relationships. But once you do, you can use this power of healing, compassion, and creative imagination toward untold ends.

Intense Attraction: **Venus in Aries or Scorpio**

In either Aries or Scorpio, Venus is in its detriment. Here, Venus has to steer your life's direction in conditions that feel opposite to its nature. This creates a natural tension that asks for extra effort from the planet. Like a captain at sea during a storm, Venus is steering the life in a compromised situation. This might not signify ease in reaching your destination, but the journey will be anything but dull. You might be someone who challenges gender norms and goes against the grain in the area of life that it is impacting (both the house that it is in and the ones it rules). Venus in its detriment may experience difficulty building and sustaining relationships but, more than that, it's important to remember that planets in their detriment tend to work harder than ones that are in their own domicile. So, while things may not be handed to you, your effort and contribution to achieving your life's purpose will eventually open up the doors you need.

VENUS IN ARIES

Since Aries is a sign that loves action and runs hot, Venus in Aries may tend to, at least in early life, burn through relationships at a fast pace. What Venus in Aries really needs is a challenge in regard to romantic or creative outlets. As ruler of your Ascendant, this might work into the themes of your life's direction and purpose. So too might the themes of being different from what society expects of you. There is a contrariness to this placement that is bold and courageous in its style. You may need to make peace with being the one who is going to challenge the status quo. Your job is to focus that energy toward positive ends for you. Aries causes conflict, and Venus wants pleasure. Sex requires friction, as do many important aspects of creativity. As long as you don't stifle your energy, anger, or desire, this placement can make you a leader with great insight, but if you deny its power and your own need for healthy stress, the destructive tendencies of the placement can run you ragged.

VENUS IN SCORPIO

Venus in Scorpio is famous for desiring intense connections that few can appreciate the depths of. With Venus in Scorpio as ruler of your Ascendant, part of your life's direction might be about experiencing these kinds of emotional embroilments or learning to channel the obsessive desire this placement signifies into your creative projects and partnerships. This placement doesn't do small talk and, as the ruler of your Ascendant, it steers your life toward activities that are investigative, deep, penetrating, and transformative. Venus in Scorpio can represent an experience of your gender in ways opposite to the expectations that the world has of it. You may have an innate understanding of the suffering that the gender binary or gender-based violence creates and this may feature in your work and activism in the world. When your Ascendant is ruled by a planet in its detriment, you will often feel like you have to try much harder to develop yourself, but rigorous effort comes with big rewards. If you have Venus in its detriment, notice what it has forced you to develop within yourself in all aspects of love and connection.

Damsel of Details: **Venus in Virgo**

In Virgo, Venus finds itself in a place where it has been stripped of its ability to enjoy pleasure for the sheer sake of it. When the ruler of your Ascendant is in the sign of its fall, as Venus is in Virgo, it can sometimes require extra work to get where you need to go. Venus in Virgo's kink is to work with great effort and efficiency. A sucker for the grind, Venus in Virgo as ruler of your Ascendant will steer your life toward exacting and detail-oriented ends, but you may not feel appreciated, seen, or noted for your efforts. Planets in their fall struggle to feel worthy. Struggle to do their job. Struggle to function in the way they are supposed to. In Virgo, Venus can put itself in an inferior position to most. Feeling disrespected and dejected, Venus in Virgo does the only thing it knows how to do. Criticize. Analyze. Separate. Categorize.

Purification is a necessary part of creating union, beauty, and alignment—something Venus in Virgo excels at. However, if you try to purify your relationships or partners by way of criticizing their flaws and features, you'll end up isolating yourself from connection and the prosperity that comes through it. Your Venus may have you working instead of playing, so you'll have to find things to achieve that feel joyous for you. Venus in Virgo will serve the temples of its desire like a priestess of the highest order.

Venus in All the Other Signs

Venus in Gemini (connecting through social interactions), Cancer (connecting through emotional bonds), Leo (connecting through passion), Sagittarius (connecting through adventure), Capricorn (connecting through common goals), and Aquarius (connecting intellectually) is fairly neutral. Venus in any of these signs will, of course, build relationships and create beauty but will do so based on the style of the sign it is in. For example, Venus in Sagittarius will want to create relationships based on adventure, a quest for the truth, and exploration.

 Reflection Questions

- Are you known for your ability to make others feel at ease? In what ways? How is this specifically related to the sign your Venus is in?

- Are you generally liked? Even if you are someone who is controversial, do you generally find ways to build bonds with others? How is this related to the sign your Venus is in?

- Are you prone to pleasing people or forgetting about your own needs? What helps you to refocus on yourself?

- Look around your life and notice all the ways in which you naturally, without thinking about it, create beauty. What power do you find in attaining the right aesthetic for your mood or current needs?

- What do beautiful things around you do to your mood?

- How can you honor Venus in your everyday life?

- Is your Venus in a strong, challenging, or neutral sign? How does the style of the sign your Venus is in speak to the ways in which you go about your life's direction?

MARS AS RULER (ARIES RISING, SCORPIO RISING)

When Mars is the ruler of your Ascendant, your life's direction is steered by a passionate, driven, sometimes aggressive, and generally courageous sentiment. Aries and Scorpio have their own distinct ways of doing this, as the section regarding your rising sign detailed, but no matter your rising sign, with Mars as the planet in charge of steering the direction of your life, you will be demonstrating your ability to tackle difficult circumstances with a great amount of energy and desire. The sign that Mars is in will tell you the specific style in which you move toward your life's main aims.

Below are explanations of Mars through the signs. Please read the description of your Mars and answer any of the questions that resonate with you.

Warrior Ways: *Mars in Aries or Scorpio*

Mars rules both Aries and Scorpio, which means Mars is at home (in its domicile) in both signs. This gives both signs an edge. If Mars works better when in one of its own signs, what exactly is it working better at? Is it more likely to do damage well, or does it desire to protect and defend? Both can be true. Being ruled by a planet that has a penchant for aggravation may mean that you have to learn how to use your power and energy to defend against what's harmful instead of unconsciously (or consciously) causing it. Though there are similarities as to how Mars works in both of its domiciles, there are some very important differences.

MARS IN ARIES

As ruler of Aries, Mars is bold. Fast and furious. Able to cut through the thick fog of fear that immobilizes most of us, Mars in Aries is the warrior in action. On the field and engaged in battle. Rushing toward its target. On the edge and pushing past it. Aries is a fire sign, and here, Mars is prone to act first and forget to ask questions later. Blazing through challenges big and little, Mars in Aries makes its mission known. If Mars in Aries rules your Ascendant, what you tackle may be done in an extreme manner, but it will get done. Knowing what you are fighting for, protecting, and serving can help you to go far with any aim. This is a tremendously strong signature to have in your chart, and it is up to you to learn and refine how you use it.

MARS IN SCORPIO

In Scorpio, Mars battles mostly in secret. As ruler of your Ascendant, Mars in Scorpio lends you its strategic powers. Long-range psychological warfare is Mars in Scorpio's forte. How you use it is entirely up to you, however. If you give a sting, you better be able to receive one in return. This combination is resilient beyond reason, and as the planet that steers your life's direction, you might be too. With Mars as ruler of your Ascendant, you'll have the patience, persistence, and ability to work through the most difficult of scenarios. You may even be drawn to them. Those around you may constantly remark on how you are able to do and say the most challenging things, but if you are carrying with you the ability to sort through the densest, funkiest, most horrific aspects of being human, what else are you going to do? Mars in Scorpio as ruler of your Ascendant will want to know what life is like at the edge and can therefore need to work with people who are too.

Warrior of Wonder: **Mars in Capricorn**

Mars is exalted in Capricorn. Here, like all exalted planets, Mars gives you a certain amount of fame for what it's good at. Known for your ability to accomplish challenging tasks, you are emboldened to constantly outdo yourself. This is a very strong placement and speaks to the life being steered toward success; whether that success makes you happy lies in your ability to direct yourself toward what is soulful and emotionally fulfilling. A worker like no other, Mars in Capricorn steers your life toward conquering your to-do list while climbing to the top of your current mountain. Calling your life's direction ambitious would be an understatement.

This placement will help you to be a leader in some regard, though Capricorn is known for being a lone wolf. With this placement you may be more than happy to go off on your own, a master of yourself.

Wounded Warriors: **Mars in Taurus or Libra**

Mars's ability to fight outright is impeded when the warrior finds itself in Taurus or Libra, the signs of its detriment. Here, Mars may get angry about things that it has every right to, but it will generally have a hard time articulating why or finding a reasonable way to remedy the situation.

Mars in its detriment defends and protects itself differently. Like all planets in their detriment, it is working in conditions opposite to its nature. When your Ascendant is ruled by a planet in its detriment, life can sometimes feel like you've gone to a pool party even though you can't swim and hate being in the Sun. It's just not your first choice, but there you are. You make the best of it, even if it's uncomfortable. You compensate. You make effort. You learn about something you wouldn't necessarily choose for yourself.

Here, Mars is less able to move with absolute certainty. Mars in its detriment has to work through second- and third-guessing itself, but when it gets to its conclusion, it will have worked hard for it and be able to own it completely.

MARS IN TAURUS

In Taurus, Mars may defend itself through inaction. Some might call this lazy, but you can't push a bull. It's not that Mars in this sign doesn't get angry or take action, it's just slow to rouse.

If Mars rules your Ascendant and it's in Taurus, life might at times feel slow to ignite, so you'll have to remind yourself that you are in it for the long haul. Nothing won in a rush is satisfying to this combination, and that sentiment might rule your life in some way. Mars in Taurus isn't going to jump into an uncomfortable situation one minute earlier than it needs to, but once in, it's in. The same goes for taking action. It can take the long road, but it's not going to veer from its path. With Mars in Taurus ruling your Ascendant, you will arrive, just on your own time.

MARS IN LIBRA

With Mars in Libra ruling your Ascendant, your best defense can often be an incredibly likable offense. Mars lives on the battlefield. Libra wants peace and harmony. With this as ruler of your Ascendant, you'll have to do battle without causing a disruption, an impossible feat that your Mars in Libra will never give up on. Possibly too forgiving at times, with Mars in Libra steering your life's direction, you'll want to win with everyone. Unable to think only of your own interests, this combination is likely to make you give your weapons to your opponents. Boundaries, therefore, become a big deal for this placement. In Libra, Mars is forced to function in a style opposite to its nature. However, some very creative possibilities can come from Mars when its focus is justice, balance, and the needs of everyone involved.

Water Wars: *Mars in Cancer*

A warrior waterlogged, Mars is in its fall in Cancer. Crabs scuttle sideways, making this version of Mars a little more prone to passive-aggressive tactics as its only option for defense. A soggy soldier, Cancer's moodiness can make its motivations emotionally muddied. With Mars in Cancer as the ruler of your Ascendant, part of your life's direction may be to find your way through the emotional ups and downs that embroil you in internal battles. Knowing what dampens your ability to effectively channel your righteous rage will help you to establish honest, emotional closeness. Cancer is a sign that wants to create stability through emotional bonds with others. Mars as ruler of your Ascendant is therefore burdened with the impossible task of defending itself without rupturing any of the connections it cares for. As with any water sign, emotion repressed can be a dangerous thing. Turning into tidal waves of stifled emotional energy, Mars in Cancer can devastate situations when it refuses itself the time and space necessary to sort through feelings that lie beneath the surface of its facade. You will need to learn how to be a warrior fighting for what needs protection as part of your life's purpose.

Mars in All the Other Signs

Mars in Gemini (sharp communicator), Leo (courageous persona), Virgo (courageous critic), Sagittarius (courageous adventurer), Aquarius (courageous intellectual), and Pisces (spiritual warrior) is fairly neutral. Mars will, of course, demonstrate its courage and desire based on the style of the sign it is in. For example, Mars in Aquarius will be potently courageous in its communications, able to cut to the core of a thought with the precision of a surgeon.

✍️ Reflection Questions

- What have you learned to effectively fight for in your life? What have been the challenges along the path of doing so?

- When does your anger, passion, or misguided energy get you in trouble? What helps you to redirect it?

- Where in your life do you find it most important or impactful to apply your energy?

- Where in your life is your ability to be contrary most effectively put to use?

- Do people often tell you that you are brave? How does that make you feel?

- Is your Mars in a strong, challenging, or neutral sign? How does the style of the sign your Mars is in speak to the ways in which you go about pursuing your life's direction?

JUPITER AS RULER
(SAGITTARIUS RISING, PISCES RISING)

♃ ☉

If you have a Sagittarius or Pisces Ascendant, Jupiter is the ruler of it. When Jupiter is the ruler of your Ascendant, your life's direction is steered by a relentless optimism and an abundance of goodwill. With an overdoing, overextending, and exuberant kind of steersperson, Jupiter in charge of your life's direction wants you to go big. Sagittarius or Pisces, as your rising sign, will each have their own distinct styles, but with Jupiter as the planet in charge of both, optimism is clearly steering the ship of your life.

Failing outright is unlikely when you are being led by Jupiter, not because you are always able to do what you set out to, or that life is fair or forgiving, but because Jupiter will always try to steer your life toward being grateful, seeing opportunity no matter the challenge, and finding the silver lining to focus on.

The sign that Jupiter is in will tell you the specific style in which you move toward your life's main aim. Below are explanations of Jupiter through the signs. Please read the description of your Jupiter and answer any of the questions that resonate with you.

Captain Fantastic: *Jupiter in Sagittarius or Pisces*

Jupiter is at home in both Sagittarius and Pisces. In either of its own signs, Jupiter creates an unwavering faith, confidence in the self, and an ability to push through the dense realities that life puts in your path. Having Jupiter in its own domicile is much like a winning lottery ticket. It is something that is easy to take for granted, as it was gifted to you by the gods. What you don't work for you often misplace, misuse, and misunderstand.

Those with Jupiter in its own sign can have a lot of lucky experiences in life, but even they need to learn how to work at creating places for it to manifest, becoming disciplined enough to understand what about it helps them to create a meaningful and fulfilling life.

JUPITER IN SAGITTARIUS

Here, Jupiter is empowered to help you bring about your life's purpose. Steered toward inspiration and the ability to act on faith, Jupiter in Sagittarius infuses your life's path with an abundance of intuitive blessings. Make sure you listen to them. The wild horses of Sagittarius want you to run freely toward many philosophical possibilities. An untamable mind is one that is focused on the truth. Seeking the ultimate expressions of it, with Jupiter in Sagittarius as your ruler, you will need to gallop toward the experiences that help you generate the best questions. This placement will always orient your life toward ever better quests.

Infused with visions of future adventures, having Jupiter in Sagittarius ruling your Ascendant means that it's important to trust your visions. Creatively, you'll need to be fearless in your explorations. You'll be led by a faith that is unrelenting, but sometimes undeservedly so. Jupiter in Sagittarius unchecked will count its chickens before it even has the eggs. Like all planets in their own signs, Jupiter in Sagittarius is extremely itself.

JUPITER IN PISCES

This creative and fertile placement knows no bounds. Jupiter in its own sign and in charge of steering your life's path gives you an advantage. You easily become a generator of opportunities for yourself and others because the nature of this signature is overflowing abundance.

But abundance isn't always easy to handle or hold.

This placement opens up opportunities for you, but you may have difficulty sorting through which to take on and an even harder time following through with them. The fluidity of Pisces engenders emotional connections with many, and here Jupiter becomes more of a consoling philosopher than a strategic guide. Your life is steered toward connecting to what you find meaningful, soulfully inspiring, and maybe even spiritually illuminating. A natural teacher, Jupiter in Pisces will lead you to give of what you have. Jupiter in Pisces does its best to connect to the pain of others, knowing that compassion is the greatest tenet to espouse. This makes alleviating a little pain when and where possible the aim and orientation of your life.

Waters of Wonder: *Jupiter in Cancer*

In Cancer, Jupiter is exalted. This is an auspicious combination that lends you the ability to manifest your blessings. Jupiter's fertility is at an all-time high in these waters, and as ruler of your Ascendant, this means that you'll be known for your ability to give, conceive of creative projects, and generally have an excess of optimism and compassion to pour forth to others. Jupiter in Cancer wants to feed, nourish, and nurture many, and as the planet that steers the direction of your life, you'll most likely have the desire to feed, symbolically or specifically, many a malnourished being.

Jupiter in Cancer knows how to protect its abundant life force so that something of note can be created. As the ruler of your Ascendant, this gives you an understanding of how to channel the most important nutrients toward what you wish to grow. You'll most likely be well known for your ability to care deeply for all you bring to life.

Magnitudes of Minutiae: **Jupiter in Gemini or Virgo**

When Jupiter is in either Gemini or Virgo, it is in its detriment. Here, Jupiter struggles. While Jupiter's home signs, Sagittarius and Pisces, focus on the big picture, the places of its detriment, Gemini and Virgo, focus on the details.

Having Jupiter both in its detriment and in charge of the direction of your life will generally implore you to work harder. In either sign, Jupiter magnifies the number of facts, data, and details in any situation. In Gemini or Virgo, Jupiter can make it difficult to discern what a sensible amount of information is, what to believe in, or how to cultivate the open, easy relationship to life that Jupiter is famous for. Jupiter in its detriment can have a lack of faith, a difficulty finding a philosophy that feels resonant, and is hard-pressed to create from a place of optimistic abundance.

Like all planets in their detriment, Jupiter in Gemini or Virgo as ruler of the Ascendant will steer the life's direction in some way that is contrary to what is expected.

JUPITER IN GEMINI

In Gemini, Jupiter has bucketloads of ideas, sentiments, and stories to tell, and as ruler of the Ascendant they need to find a home. This placement can make someone more than curious and willing to share insights and discoveries with the world. With an unending flood of facts, Jupiter in Gemini can have a hard time getting to the point, for what good is a point when you're surrounded by interesting tidbits that send you into far-off corners of your mind? What this might mean in terms of your life's direction is that, intentionally or unintentionally, you get sidetracked. Encumbered with fragments of the truth, Jupiter as ruler of the Ascendant can lead you off course, but getting back on track will be part of the muscle that you must build. Doing so will give you a tremendous strength and clarity about how to live a life that feels like it's moving in a soulful and satisfying direction.

JUPITER IN VIRGO

In Virgo, Jupiter's optimism is often interrupted by constant critique. Virgo is a sign that gets mired in the details, and here as ruler of your Ascendant, Jupiter can tend to have you magnifying all the impurities, flaws, and imperfections to fret over. Phobias can tend to overwhelm your ability to find solutions and strategies. Jupiter's natural ability to make possibilities out of bleak positions is low functioning when it's in Virgo. As ruler of your Ascendant, this placement increases your appetite for work, making you a force of industriousness, but when overly focused on the small stuff, you'll have a hard time creating something that is abundant in and of itself.

Luck may feel evasive, but place your awareness on incremental growth. Having Jupiter in Virgo may lead you to feel devalued in academic, spiritual, or philosophical circles, but finding company in alternative spaces where your philosophies are appreciated will be satiating and perhaps even the point of your life's direction.

Conservative Growth: *Jupiter in Capricorn*

In Saturn's sign, Jupiter is in its fall. Like all planets in their fall, a kind of disrespect is paid to Jupiter in this sign. As the ruler of your Ascendant, this may have you feeling the same in some situations or early in life. Constrained by Capricorn's austere style, the planet that steers the direction of your life makes you cautious of growth and expansion, though it is clearly part of your life's direction. Here Jupiter is more skeptical, conservative in its ability to expend energy, and unwilling to risk its reputation for fear of looking foolish. It will therefore cause a natural tension in your ability to grow, develop your ideas, and heal as your life needs you to. Jupiter struggles to find the buoyancy it would otherwise embody and as the ruler of your Ascendant, it might have you wondering why things aren't a little easier to attain.

However, Jupiter in Capricorn does have a system of checks and balances, something that Jupiter in its own domicile does not have. In Capricorn, Jupiter will not be fooled by the fleeting nature of the wheel of fortune. It would rather feel the satisfaction of its well-earned accomplishments than depend on luck that may or may not strike it rich. This placement makes you strive to understand how hard work meets opportunity, and when it does, what doors you know for sure you can carry yourself through.

Jupiter in All the Other Signs

Jupiter in Aries (courageous expansion), Taurus (steady, generative growth), Leo (expansion though self-expression), Libra (abundant harmony), Scorpio (deep expansion), and Aquarius (expansive ideas) is fairly neutral. Jupiter in any of these signs will, of course, create opportunities for growth and expansion based on the style of the sign it is in. For example, Jupiter in Libra will use your ability to connect and initiate relationships as a means to create your good fortune.

☑ Reflection Questions

- Where in your life are you able to demonstrate a boundless faith or optimism? What doors does it open for you?

- Where in your life is it important for you to be expansive? What are your obstacles in doing so? Who or what tends to tell you to shrink?

- Do others find you inspiring? What is it that they usually comment on as being so? How does it make you feel?

- What do you tend to overdo in your life? How have you come to accept this about yourself? Is there a balance to be found?

- Is what you work on often large in size or scope? When does it feel overwhelming?

- Is your Jupiter in a strong, challenging, or neutral sign? How does the style of the sign your Jupiter is in speak to the ways in which you go about pursuing your life's direction?

SATURN AS RULER
(CAPRICORN RISING, AQUARIUS RISING)

ħ ☉

If you have a Capricorn or Aquarius Ascendant, Saturn is its ruler. When Saturn is the ruler of your Ascendant, your life's direction is steered by self-restraint, a sense of responsibility, and a need to accomplish something that is worth your efforts and hard work. Saturn is a planet that demands your best and, as ruler of your Ascendant, will want nothing less than a life that leads you toward self-mastery, autonomy, and hard-earned accolades. Sometimes with Saturn as ruler of your Ascendant, you don't feel at ease until you are older. As the planet that governs age, authority, and maturity, Saturn demands that you spend time developing yourself.

The most distant planet that the naked eye can see is Saturn. It has a penchant for being standoffish, even aloof, but it's not because it is uncaring. With Saturn as your ruler, you may be happy in your solitude, as it allows you to get your work done, but that doesn't mean you don't need others.

Because Saturn tends toward discrimination and discernment, unless something else in the chart says otherwise, your life's direction will be sought after in a style that can involve a fair amount of self-denial. Saying no is a powerful statement, but when you say no to yourself unfairly, that harshness can spill over into the rest of your relationships. When Saturn is ruler of your Ascendant, you'll need to master the art of what to refuse and what to allow. Your yeses will come more easily when you know what boundaries to hold firm and which to soften.

Below are explanations of Saturn through the signs. Please read the description of your Saturn and answer any of the questions that resonate with you.

Master of Ceremonies: Saturn in Capricorn or Aquarius

Saturn is at home in Capricorn and Aquarius. When the ruler of your Ascendant is in its own sign, it is a signification of strength and clear direction in life. It is something that you can lean on when life gets rough. It's something that, if you develop a relationship to it, will not forsake you. To radically accept yourself is to know what to ally with and what to interrupt and unpack.

Saturn in its own sign is a resource readily available to you. Its gifts include self-discipline, scrutiny, and an ability to suffer through what is uncomfortable in order to attain what is admirable. Saturn isn't here for immediate gratification, and if this planet steers your life's direction, it's beneficial for you to take the same stance. Think about what you can develop over decades. Think about what will help you feel the kind of satisfaction that sinks into your bones. Think about what you could spend your lifetime working on, no matter the ups or downs of it, that would be worth your energy, passion, and pursuit.

SATURN IN CAPRICORN

As ruler of Capricorn, Saturn is the keeper of tradition. As the ruler of your Ascendant, it's important for you to know which traditions you want to keep and which would be structurally unwise. Here, Saturn knows the importance of understanding the original shape, meaning, and reasoning of a thing. As ruler of your Ascendant, Saturn wants to make you known for your ability to manifest your desires into the physical world through discipline, structure building, and a sturdy, steady, reliable work ethic. The more you can develop a relationship to these attributes in your own unique, specific way, the more you'll feel aligned with your purpose. If Saturn is your ruler, the last thing you want to be known for is being unwilling to try your best.

SATURN IN AQUARIUS

In Aquarius, Saturn learns all the rules, inside and out, so that it can break them with efficiency as needed. Aquarius is not messy. It's not a rebel without a cause. Its intellect is exacting. As the ruler of your Ascendant, Saturn wants you to channel the same. You'll need to buck a system, but not without measured consideration. Saturn wants you to develop your understanding of how best to redistribute and decentralize power. Aquarius is a gifted observer. With Saturn as ruler, you might be known for your intellectual detachment, but understanding a situation from as many angles as possible is essential if you are to follow the direction of your life's path.

Discerning Style: **Saturn in Libra**

In Libra, Saturn is exalted and, as ruler of your Ascendant, will lend you recognition for your mature, even-keeled nature. Being known for your ability to work hard, be disciplined, and make conservative but well-measured decisions can help you become a fair and respected master of your craft. Saturn in Libra makes you an approachable authority, gives you a likable style, and will steer you to seek justice in the structures you build or work within. This ruler helps you make distinctions without being discourteous, and you'll likely be acknowledged for your fair and even approach.

Captain Eeyore: *Saturn in Cancer or Leo*

Saturn is in its detriment in Cancer and Leo. Like all planets in their detriment, Saturn struggles to find its way in these signs. Being ruled by the planet associated with self-restraint and self-mastery is pretty straightforward, but when that planet feels out of sorts, you might wonder where to put your wisdom or why it isn't appreciated. Saturn's whole focus is to be in control, but in these signs that isn't so easy. Extra effort is required of you. You'll need to earn the respect you crave, even if you do in fact already deserve it. Bruised egos and hurt feelings might be pervasive, but they must not impede your life's direction. What these placements can supply you with are ample opportunities to be humbled and do the work for its own sake, for your own satisfaction, and for your own self-respect.

SATURN IN CANCER

In Cancer, Saturn has a hard time building and maintaining the boundaries that are helpful for growth. We need to be solid in some places but permeable in others, and Saturn in Cancer can confuse the two, and issues of emotional control can abound. Part of your life's journey might be to stifle your emotions as a means to control life. This is an understandable defense mechanism but not one that is helpful in the long run. You may also tend to be overcome with emotions, unable or unwilling to build the structures that you need to hold your experience. Saturn-ruled people tend to have a harder time in their younger life. Age brings a kind of comfort and wisdom that Saturn feels more dignified in. In Cancer, Saturn's hard shell can protect you from being permeated by important reflections or much-needed feedback. Defensiveness becomes a thorn in the side of those ruled by Saturn in Cancer, impeding your ability to flourish. You need to learn to hold space for your feelings without trying to control your emotional life. If you can do so, you will become an insightful guide for others in their own healing journey.

SATURN IN LEO

In Leo, a sign where Saturn finds itself in its detriment, the taskmaster is asked to tend to its duties in a dramatic fashion. This is a strange sentiment for a planet known for its cool demeanor. Gaining applause is not Saturn's game. This planet conserves, but Leo has endless energy to burn and wants nothing to do with downplaying its talent. With Saturn in Leo as the ruler of your Ascendant, you'll have to find ways to demonstrate your diligence, discipline, and self-mastery so that it gets you attention but not the kind that is frivolous or fleeting. Saturn wants longlasting results. Saturn in the sign known for its magnanimous and self-centered approach to life struggles to be taken seriously or struggles with too rigid an ego identification.

The main difficulty of a planet in detriment is that it is unable to complete its task easily or in the way that it is "supposed to." Therefore, Saturn in its detriment can steer your life toward managing authority differently. You may have difficulty juggling the need for accolades with the need to feel like you have earned them. You'll need to know that your ego won't corrupt your integrity.

When Saturn in Leo steers the ship of your life, you must learn how best to become your own authority—society's rules and your family norms be damned.

Fire Walls: **Saturn in Aries**

Saturn in its fall has you struggling to strike a balance between harsh limits and burning down all borders that keep you safe. Like all planets in their fall, Saturn in Aries feels demoted. As ruler of your Ascendant, it may make you may feel like you have to prove something about your own worth, your own abilities, and your own value through discipline and self-control. In Aries, Saturn has to work through issues of heat and anger. Tempers are hard to moderate, but if stifled, they'll eventually explode. Fast to act, Saturn in Aries can have you erecting boundaries before you have fully inspected what should be rejected or included. Like all planets in their fall, Saturn in Aries asks that you work overtime to understand the nuances between self-discipline and self-denial. Solitude and isolation. Self-respect and self-sabotage. The reward of doing so is owning your power and knowing precisely what you want to do with it.

Saturn in All Other Signs

Saturn in Taurus (self-mastery through patience and persistence), Gemini (self-mastery through developing intellect), Virgo (self-mastery through discernment), Scorpio (self-mastery through connecting with the mysteries of sex and death), Sagittarius (self-mastery through personal freedom), and Pisces (self-mastery through creative and spiritual discipline) is fairly neutral. Sat-

urn in any of these signs will, of course, build necessary structures and demonstrate self-mastery based on the style of the sign
it is in. For example, Saturn in Scorpio knows how to navigate
through the intense emotional experiences of sex, death, and
power dynamics.

Reflection Questions

- What do you generally tend to deny yourself? When is this helpful? When is it detrimental?

- Where in your life are you able to create healthy boundaries? When in life do you tend to limit or restrict your experience of intimacy?

- Are you known for being the responsible, reliable, dependable person in most situations? How does this make you feel? What do you get out of this role? What does it take from you?

- What are you most determined to achieve in life no matter what you'll need to go without?

- What do you most want to master in yourself and in your work?

- Is your Saturn in a strong, challenging, or neutral sign? How does the style of the sign your Saturn is in speak to the ways in which you go about pursuing your life's direction?

HOUSE OF YOUR ASCENDANT RULER
WHAT AREA OF LIFE ARE YOU BEING
STEERED TOWARD?

What House Is Your Ascendant Ruler In?

The house that your Ascendant ruler is in tells you what area of life you are being steered toward. Without developing a relationship to this house, you will not feel fulfilled. Recall that Frida Kahlo had a Leo Ascendant. Her flair for decorative self-expression was undeniable. Leo is the performer, the creatrix, the one who lives out some aspect of the human experience for all to witness. Her Leo Ascendant articulated her motivation for living: to be fiery, creatively potent, and seen. Moreover, the sign of her Sun, Cancer, reveals that she was steered by a planet whose style was emotive. The house her Sun was in tells us about the area of life she needed to explore in order to connect to her life's purpose. Her Sun lived in the 12th House of sorrows, loss, hidden life, secrets, and the collective unconscious.

When Frida Kahlo was six, she contracted polio. Bedridden for months, her right leg would never grow to the same size as her left leg. At eighteen, she experienced a much more serious physical trauma. In a near-fatal bus accident, a steel handrail came loose and impaled her womb, leaving her spine broken in three places, and her right leg, the one impacted by polio, shattered. She was not expected to live. During her recovery she was forced to wear a full body cast for three months. Unable to move, she was encouraged by her parents to take up painting. They created an easel that she could use in bed, gave her supplies, and fashioned a mirror so she could create self-portraits.

The physical and emotional suffering that Kahlo endured is not simply the result of having her Sun in the 12th House of sorrow, isolation, and loss (she also had Mars, sharp and cutting, and Uranus, unpredictable and disruptive, opposing her Sun). However, expressing this pain through her art and writing is, in an astrological context, what her life steered her toward. Kahlo famously said, "I paint myself because I am often alone, and I am the subject I know best."* If your Ascendant ruler is in the 12th House, it does not necessarily mean you will suffer, but it does mean that addressing suffering, the most human of conditions, is a main theme of your life's direction and purpose.

 Now it is time to choose your own adventure. Please skip ahead to the house that the ruler of your Ascendant, or your rising sign, lives in.

ASCENDANT RULER IN THE 1ST HOUSE

Body, appearance, self, life force

If the planet that rules your Ascendant is in the 1st House, the significations of that planet and all it governs will be extra active in your life. This is true for two reasons. First, any planet in the 1st House will be prominently expressed through your identity, personality, and physical self. Second, if the ruler of your Ascendant is in the 1st House, it will be in its own sign and act in a straightforward, clear, and direct manner. This combination is strong and may even be extreme. The ruler of your Ascendant, and all it stands for, is being asked to be woven into your identity. For

---

*Frida Kahlo Foundation; see www.frida-kahlo-foundation.org.

example, if Jupiter is your ruler and it is also in the 1st House, you are being asked to live out your life in an optimistic way, sharing your wealth and abundance of spirit with others. The ruler of the Ascendant in the 1st House is also telling you that the main focus of your life's direction is the development of your identity.

Reflection Questions

- Given the nature of the planet and the style of the sign, what themes do you notice are dominant in your life?

- When do you feel seen by others? What are you being recognized for when you feel most understood? What parts of your identity do you feel people focus too heavily on? Is that related to the planet that rules your Ascendant? Is it sometimes overwhelming to embody this so strongly?

- What parts of your personality do you feel are most misunderstood by the world? How does this relate to the planet that rules your Ascendant?

- How have you learned to push back against what feels like an imposition on you? How does the ruler of your Ascendant help or hinder this? For example, Venus might be uncomfortable doing so, as it's a planet that wants to create connection, not disrupt it, but Mars would be more comfortable being combative when necessary.

- Can you imagine the ruler of your Ascendant as free to express itself outside cultural norms?

ASCENDANT RULER IN THE 2ND HOUSE

Money, assets, resources, self-worth

We all have something to give this world. We all have some way of supporting ourselves. We all have some talent or specific ability to put to use. Our assets help us make our way through the material realm. The 2nd House details these riches. Having the ruler of your Ascendant in the 2nd House makes clear that your life's direction needs to move toward developing your resources and learning how to support yourself with them. Money and assets aren't more or less easy to come by with your ruler in the 2nd House; that all depends on the sign that the ruler of your Ascendant is in and the aspects made to it. But we know that this is a place you must develop a relationship to in order to feel fully expressed in this life.

✍ Reflection Questions

- How do you see your life's purpose as being tied directly to your assets and ability to develop them?

- What about the nature of the planet that rules your Ascendant makes an obvious manifestation in your work? For example, if Mars rules your Ascendant and Mars is in your 2nd House, do you engage in work where you have to fight, perhaps on behalf of others?

- What about the style of the sign that the planet is in? For example, if the Moon rules your Ascendant and the Moon is in your 2nd House, it will be in Leo. Is part of your livelihood (2nd House) about nurturing others (Moon) through creativity and self-expression (Leo)?

ASCENDANT RULER IN THE 3RD HOUSE

Communication, siblings, extended family, close friends,
daily life and rituals, the House of Goddess

If the ruler of your Ascendant is in your 3rd House, your life's direction points to developing relationships, communications, and daily and spiritual rituals. Specifically, writing, teaching, delivering information, working with family or good friends, performing or holding space for devotional practices, studying or teaching about the Goddess or other ancient religious traditions that predate monotheism, traveling (especially throughout the day and around your neighborhood), and being in contact with many folks during the day are some of the ways in which you will feel like you are on track.

The 3rd House is the place of the Moon's joy. If, for example, you have Cancer rising, the Moon is the ruler of your Ascendant. If you have the Moon in Virgo and in the 3rd House, then the moon is both the ruler of your Ascendant and in the place of its joy. That gives extra strength to the ruler of your Ascendant and its ability to do its job. The Moon is always strong in the 3rd House whether or not your Ascendant is Cancer, but if it's also the ruler of your Ascendant, it's a blessing to take note of.

Reflection Questions

- How is your life energy directed toward communication, writing, teaching, or travel? How is your life shaped by these activities?

- What roles do your siblings, friends, and extended family play in the direction of your life? Do their ups and downs impact you greatly? Do they dictate your life in any way? Are you in partnership with them?

- Do you work in communities and neighborhoods or are you involved with them in any significant way?

- Is your life focused on rituals, especially those that are spiritual? Do you find that you are usually the person who brings rituals or a sense of spirituality to others' lives?

- What about the nature of the planet that rules your Ascendant makes an obvious manifestation in your communications? For example, if Venus rules your Ascendant and Venus is in your 3rd House, are you known for being someone who delivers a message with sweetness?

ASCENDANT RULER IN THE 4TH HOUSE

Foundation of all things, ancestry,
home, family, parents

Having the ruler of your Ascendant in the 4th House reveals that how you physically and aesthetically create home, who you create it with, and how you carry forth the traditions of your people, matter deeply to you. If the ruler of your Ascendant is here, one or more of these issues will be a prominent part of how you manifest your life's direction. You may notice that you come up against issues related to how to honor family traditions and your lineage without getting stuck in the past. Balancing commitment to family while being able to break ties with the aspects of your origin stories that don't support you may be a main theme in your life.

Without understanding your 4th House, it's difficult to build any long-lasting structures in your life. Without understanding what you need from an inner life, it's difficult to build an outer life that will be fulfilling. If you can dig into the past and unpack its meaning, heal the wounds there, and come to understand your unique contribution to the lineages you hail from, then you will be more likely to build a healthy relationship with the present.

📝 Reflection Questions

- How does the nature of the planet that rules your Ascendant speak to the relationship that you have with your immediate family or with your family in general?

- What do you feel drawn to honor and carry through in your lineage? What do you feel the need to break away from?

- Do you ever find it difficult to do something that is different from what your family does or to satisfy their hopes for your life or future?

- What about the nature of the planet that rules your Ascendant makes an obvious manifestation in your family life? For example, if Jupiter rules your Ascendant and it is in your 4th House, is there some blessing, abundance, or spirituality that comes from family? Is one of your parents larger than life? If it's a more difficult planet, like Mars, was one of your parents daring or courageous? Does dealing with harm or being uprooted and severed from your roots play a large role in your life's purpose?

ASCENDANT RULER IN THE 5TH HOUSE

Children, creative and erotic energy, pleasure, fun, romance, sex

We all create our own lives every day. Through your actions, through your speech, through your agreements and your decisions, you constantly create your life. If the ruler of your Ascendant is in the 5th House, your creative energy and how you manifest it become central themes in your life and major areas of importance. When the ruler of the Ascendant is here, your life is steered toward taking the energy you have been given and implementing it in the world consciously and deliberately.

Traditionally known as the house of children, this part of the chart indicates fertility. If the ruler of your Ascendant is here and it is placed in a strong sign, your life will most likely be governed by generativity. The ruler of the Ascendant in the 5th House generally wants to produce. Since children were seen as necessary blessings in the ancient world, the 5th House is also known as the place of good fortune.

This is the house where Venus has its joy. Venus, planet of pleasure, erotic energy, and all things that are fun and enjoyable, knows how to have a good time in this house. If you are Taurus or Libra rising and your Venus is in the 5th House, it is extra potent, as Venus is incredibly comfortable here. Life is then dominated by beauty, desire, and fun.

Reflection Questions

- How do art, creativity, and self-expression dominate your life?

- How does working with, for, or having children help you to live out your life's purpose?

- Are you someone who is known for being the life of the party, having a good time, or being able to land yourself in good fortune?

- Does your good fortune sometimes inhibit you from pushing yourself, working hard, or moving through difficulties?

- What about the nature of the planet that rules your 1st House makes an obvious manifestation in your relationship with creativity? For example, if the Moon rules your 1st House and it's in your 5th House, are you known for nurturing creative projects or children? Are you someone who works within the realm of reproductive health?

ASCENDANT RULER IN THE 6TH HOUSE

Work projects, work habits, work schedules, pets,
health matters, accidents, illness

Having the ruler of your Ascendant in the 6th House means that you will find a sense of purpose and personal fulfillment through your work life and your professional routines.

In traditional astrology, this is the house that deals with slavery, theft of labor, and human trafficking. Work and the pursuit of it can dominate your energy, time, and attention. You may find that balance in this area is hard to come by. The people you are closest to may need to work with you in order to be part of your world. It may be challenging for you to relax and unwind at times, as you may be more comfortable being productive than pursuing pleasure and connections. As such, working toward just and equitable employment conditions can be an important aspect of your journey and life.

This is also the place of pets and livestock. With your Ascendant ruler here, you may have an affinity for animals or work with them.

Because this is the house of illness, some with their Ascendant ruler in the 6th House will either work with those who live with illness, chronic or otherwise, or experience it themselves in a way that defines their life.

📝 Reflection Questions

- Is your life's direction steered toward working in health care, the healing industry, or with those who have a hard time due to health issues?

- Is work important to your sense of self?

- Do you tend to overwork or overidentify with your work?

- Do you sometimes feel a loss of power in regard to your work situation?

- Do you work with others who have experienced or are experiencing oppressive work environments?

- What about the nature of the planet that rules your 1st House makes an obvious manifestation in your work projects? For example, if Mercury rules your 1st House and it's in your 6th House, does your work life depend heavily on your ability to communicate, translate, write, teach, or sell?

ASCENDANT RULER IN THE 7TH HOUSE

Committed partnerships, marriage, business relationships,
clients, open enemies

To have your Ascendant ruler in the 7th House makes committed partnerships, business relationships, and the lessons that they bring incredibly important to your life's purpose. Planets in the 7th House are extra active, because of the strength of the house (the 1st, 4th, 7th, and 10th houses are the strongest houses). What your partners go through impacts your life in obvious ways. Given the power of your bond with people you're in relationship with, make sure that you commit to those who know how to be good partners, friends, change agents, and catalysts for you. That way you'll be in alignment with what you most need and what is most beneficial for you.

There may be times in your life where an overemphasis on others is apparent. When the ruler of the 1st House is in the 7th, it will, by default, be a planet in the sign of its detriment. That is because the 7th House is the opposite house from the first, and any planet across from its own sign is sitting in territory that feels contrary to its nature. This begs the question, if your life's direction is always moving toward the activities of another, do you lose sight of your own needs? It is of extra importance that you seek out the relationships that feel most aligned with your purpose, as it is in partnership that you achieve it.

Reflection Questions

- How have your most significant relationships or committed partnerships impacted the direction of your life?

- Do you often forgo your own needs to make others happy?

- Do you feel driven to find partnerships that allow you to do what you can't do on your own?

- Who in your life helps you to access and activate your life's purpose?

- What have you learned about taking care of yourself through your significant partnerships?

- Which partnerships have brought you success, fame, or recognition?

- What is it about the nature of the planet that rules your Ascendant that makes an obvious manifestation in your committed partnerships? For example, if Saturn rules your 1st House and it's in your 7th House, do you tend to attract partners who are responsible, reliable, committed, critical, discerning, or emotionally remote? Do you tend to project your authority onto them, making them into taskmasters instead of taking responsibility for your life and choices?

ASCENDANT RULER IN THE 8TH HOUSE

Collaborations, other people's money and assets,
inheritances, death, mental anguish, grief

The Ascendant ruler in the 8th House steers the direction of your life toward important collaborations. Those with this placement can become skilled producers, managers, bankers, or accountants, and generally do well in any situation where they can take the product or resource of another and make the world aware of it.

Since this is also the house of death, grief, and loss, the Ascendant ruler in the 8th House can steer you toward working with these difficult aspects of life. Grief counselors, death doulas, mental health experts, therapists, exorcists, past-life regressionists, and any occupation that makes contact with the spirit world would be a fit for people with an Ascendant ruler in the 8th House.

Certain near-death experiences may also have defined your life and set you on a path of purpose or understanding. The death of loved ones, especially those who changed your life, would also be related to this placement.

✍ Reflection Questions

- Is your life steered toward working collaboratively? To do so, what do you have to learn about what you bring to the table? What are you learning to receive?

- Do you rely on the money, assets, or resources of others, and if so where is your power in that situation?

- Does some major part of your work have to do with funding, grants, or loans (giving or receiving)?

- Do you feel a connection with the spirit realm, the other side, or with the death and dying process?

- What near-death experiences have shaped you and changed the direction of your life?

- What about the nature of the planet that rules your Ascendant makes an obvious manifestation in your work? For example, if the Sun rules your 1st House and it's in your 8th House, do you shine in collaborations? Do you identify with the more mysterious elements of life?

ASCENDANT RULER IN THE 9TH HOUSE

Travel, teaching, publishing, philosophy, law, spirituality, religion, astrology, the House of God

Having your Ascendant ruler in the 9th House makes your life direction the pursuit of meaning. Here, you need adventure, want to seek knowledge and wisdom, and will need to practice the art of teaching, learning, and putting your ideas out into the world. In the 9th House, planets are driven to gather insight through experience. You may or may not undertake graduate work, a degree, or a certificate, but the process of learning will always be a place where you feel inspired.

Because there is a certain spiritual quality associated with the 9th House, if your Ascendant ruler is here, you might feel drawn to, or repelled from, certain religious customs or institutions. Whatever the experience, it will play a part in shaping your life.

✏️ Reflection Questions

- Are you someone who lives in a different country from the one you were born in?

- Does traveling fill you with a sense of purpose?

- Does teaching connect you to something meaningful?

- Do you spend a lot of your life in academic institutions?

- Is your life driven by the seeking of truth, wisdom, and meaning?

- What about the nature of the planet that rules your 1st House makes an obvious manifestation in your studies, philosophies, publishing, and travel? For example, if Venus rules your 1st House and it's in your 9th House, do you study or teach gender studies, women's studies, queer history, or anything related?

ASCENDANT RULER IN THE 10TH HOUSE

Career, public and professional roles

If your Ascendant ruler is in your 10th House, you are directed to pursue professional and public roles. The 10th House is one of the strongest houses in the chart, and any planet here is visible and active in your life. This is the part of your chart that is the public self, and if the ruler of the Ascendant is here, it means that your life is, in part, geared toward pursuing your talents in professional spheres.

Through your career and public roles, you will find the most important struggles, triumphs, and realizations. Whether your audience is large or small matters not. What does matter is that you accept the challenge of pursuing your dreams and taking up space in the world. Public roles are where you get to connect to your purpose and are aspects of life that you should not shy away from, as they will most likely feel fulfilling.

📝 *Reflection Questions*

- Does the pursuit of your career take up much of your life's energy?

- Do you find that many of your relationships are oriented around your career or public roles?

- What are the most important public roles that you occupy?

- Does the pursuit of your career come at the cost of anything else in your life?

- What does pursuing your professional or public roles help you to realize about yourself?

- What about the nature of the planet that rules your Ascendant makes an obvious manifestation in your work? For example, if Jupiter rules your 1st House and it's in your 10th House, are you an educator? Do you inhabit public roles that are big, expansive, or spiritual?

ASCENDANT RULER IN THE 11TH HOUSE

Community, supporters, patrons, hopes and dreams for the future, good fortune through networks

With the ruler of your Ascendant in the 11th House, much of the direction of your life will have to do with the networks, movements, and organizations that you partner with. Here, your life's direction is steered toward the development of your role in the groups you feel most connected to. For some, that will be easy; for others challenging; for most, a mixture of both. The main takeaway here is that you need to develop a conscious relationship to the groups that you contribute your energy to.

With your Ascendant ruler in the 11th House, it's also important to put yourself in good company. If the group is moving in a direction that you don't want to go, parting ways is a must. Since this placement can both influence the group and be influenced by it, it's important to join peers who positively encourage your growth, challenge you to do better, and inspire you to dream without inhibition.

The 11th House is also the place where we encounter the good fortune of gathering with those who help us find love, work, and purpose. If your Ascendant ruler is in your 11th House, friends, allies, and community are most likely sources of fortune for you. Friends introduce you to important people in your life and invite you to spaces, places, and partnerships that help you in monumental ways. The quality of the help of course depends on the kind of planet and its placement in your chart.

Reflection Questions

- When you look back at your life, what social roles, group dynamics, and collective projects have been most influential for you?

- What opportunities have come to you through the friendships that have defined you in some important way?

- How do you feel your life's direction is steered by your social roles and the collectives that you become a part of?

- What about the nature of the planet that rules your 1st House makes an obvious manifestation in your community, friend groups, and hopes and dreams for the future? For example, if

Mars rules your 1st House and it's in your 11th House, do you find that you are drawn to those who rally around a cause? Is activism a big part of your life? Do you tend to be drawn to working with groups but also have some difficulty in them because you are so independent? Do you often find yourself in contentious community relationships?

ASCENDANT RULER IN THE 12TH HOUSE

Hidden life, solitude, secrets, sorrows, self-undoing,
creative energy bound up in our pain

If your Ascendant ruler is in your 12th House, the direction of your life will focus on unpacking the secrets of a situation or on the behind-the-scenes work of whatever interests you. The 12th House is the place where things are hidden. It encapsulates all the institutions in which a society places, houses, or hides its people who have either been exiled from society or who, for whatever reason, cannot integrate into it. Systems of incarceration, rehab centers, hospitals, and mental health facilities are all found in the 12th House. So are creative incubators, studios, dark rooms, and places to sit in solitude and create.

The 12th House points to the sorrow, difficulty, and pain that the psyche struggles with. Having the ruler of your 1st House in the 12th House can often lead to self-sabotage and self-undoing. If you have this placement, you'll need to learn how to interrupt these patterns so that you can experience the other aspects of this house. When you give yourself the space to sort through and unpack the trauma that you carry, you will find a source of profound creative energy.

Reflection Questions

- Do you need time alone and in incubators to connect with your creative energy? Do you value this time?

- Does your work require you to remove yourself from your social life and roles?

- Are you more comfortable in the background or behind the scenes than you are in the spotlight?

- Have you dealt with mental health institutions or the incarceration system?

- What about the nature of the planet that rules your Ascendant makes an obvious manifestation in your inner life, behind-the-scenes work, and life story? For example, if Venus rules your 1st House and it's in your 12th House, are you drawn to working with women, femmes, and gender-nonconforming folks who suffer as a result of systemic oppression? Are you someone who excavates the forgotten or hidden histories of women and gender-nonconforming folks? Do you feel that you have suffered personally because of patriarchal and gender-based violence? Having a benefic like Venus or Jupiter in the 12th House can also signify having a gift here, making it less difficult in some regard.

WHAT'S NEXT

As with any body of knowledge, a talent for working with astrology and your birth chart comes through your ability to integrate it, and that takes time. This is the frustration that so many can feel when looking at the overwhelming amount of information in their chart. What we have done in this book is review the foundations of your chart, and my hope is that you'll feel a little more secure about what you are looking at and what it all means.

Without the three keys in place, the rest of our chart tends to run amuck in our minds, but with them we are anchored in context. With the understanding that so much of the meaning of the chart is wrapped up in the placement of the luminaries (Sun and Moon), Ascendant (rising sign), and ruler (planet that rules the Ascendant), we are able to understand why some things have been easy and others challenging.

After going through the steps in this book, you'll quickly be able to see if there are any remaining planets that aren't part of

254 // YOU WERE BORN FOR THIS

the three keys. Any planets not in relationship to the Sun, Moon, Ascendant, or its ruler will still hold important information for you to work with, but (most likely) they become the supporting actors in the play of your life.*

Since we have spent so much time with Dr. Maya Angelou and Frida Kahlo, two people who have the type of cultural impact that few do, it's important to note that they lived out a kind of archetypal experience for the rest of us to witness and see ourselves reflected in. Their work speaks to their specific experience in a universal way. We can view their charts as both the personal expression of their life's purpose and the archetypal impact they had on their communities, their professional fields, and the world at large.

Dr. Maya Angelou and Frida Kahlo left the world a better place for having been in it and their lives continue to be a resource to investigate as well as a foundation to build upon politically, culturally, and artistically. We may not all experience the same level of fame or mastery of our craft, but we never know the impression we make on others. Through an astrological lens, we can come to understand how important it is to follow the path laid out before us—its impact, however, is both beyond our control and really none of our business. Studying the charts of these two is made easier because the archetypes of the planets in them so clearly proclaimed themselves through all they did and all they left behind. The study of their lives, choices, and charts can help us to understand the many ways the planets create the infrastructure of our lives. We have choice within that infrastructure, but the bones cannot be changed.

Readings from a trusted astrologer are important next steps

---

*There are other rulers in the traditional system that aren't covered here but that are important when determining the quality and direction of a life.

on your journey. Something inherently healing occurs when another person who is skilled at what they do holds space for us and can reflect our journey back to us. I still get a reading once a year from Demetra George and will continue to do so until she refuses me. That hour-long reading is an important addition to what I already know for myself. She always offers context and depth to my life's events that I miss when I rely only on my own understanding of my chart.

However, no one knows me like I do, and because of that, it is my job to take the information any astrologer gives me and find ways to put it to work. Getting readings from trained professionals is important and beneficial for your learning and healing, but only you can go in depth with your chart. Like reading a map, your chart reveals to you where to go for restoration, stimulation, activation, and satisfaction.

I want you to understand and then own the meaning, impact, and power of your chart. I and other astrologers can help you get there, but ultimately it is yours to unpack over your lifetime.

Understanding the specifics of my chart helped me fully commit to the work that was mine to do. Refusing to ignore my gifts any longer is quite literally how I came to write this book. After years of doubting the relevance of my connection to astrology and writing in general, I was able to reclaim my energy from lifelong self-doubt and redirect it toward the creative possibilities that were, and are, awaiting me. My hope is that this book helps you, in some small or large way, to do the same.

ACKNOWLEDGMENTS

I have had the good fortune of learning from many great teachers in my life, people who entered into my world at the precise moment I needed their guidance. I am the summation of their care, protection, and love. Any wisdom that I have been able to cultivate is because of the emotional, intellectual, and spiritual labor they offered me, and this book would never have been written without them.

To my mom, Teo Nicholas, whose zest for life and unstoppable energy is always rooting for me. I feel it always and appreciate it endlessly.

To my father, Tony Nicholas, who always paid me to read everyone's chart. Thank you for being my first customer and a champion of my profession. I learned the value of working from you—maybe a little too well.

To my sister, Lyndi Nedelec, who has a giant heart, the voice of an angel, and the capacity to care like few others. Thank you for always loving me exactly as I am, in ways only a little sister can. You've helped me to heal some of my deepest sorrows.

Cass, your ability to witness my journey, hold my story, and reflect it back to me with such care, clarity, and humor is one of the great gifts of my life. I would not be the person I am today without you. Thank you for telling me how the energy shifted in the room each time I spoke about astrology. You helped me trust it, you helped me connect to it, you helped me build a home in this world for my professional and adult self while never taking your eye off my inner self. What I have learned in my sessions with you has been woven into every horoscope I've ever written or will write. If people love the work, they love you too, just as I do.

Keri Lassalle, you have been a cheerleader for me from the start. You've never let me forget who I am and how sacred this work is. When I had no faith in myself, I borrowed yours in me, and it carried me through.

Eliza Melody Walter, you've been the best friend I've ever had. The place I have for you in my heart no one else could occupy. Thank you for always seeing me. Thank you for a million late nights with a billion fascinating things to pontificate upon. Our talks are lifelong and give me such solace and joy.

Ulrike Balke, thank you for taking my homemade cookies as payment for reiki sessions for the better part of a decade. You always provided a space for me to sort out my feelings, feel my body, and honor my process. Your wisdom and guidance were an anchor I held on to in times that were turbulent and confusing. I wish everyone the kind of spiritual godmother you have always been to me.

Demetra George, there are people who spend their time here on earth so immersed in conversation with a body of knowledge, with or without praise for their efforts, that they become an intrinsic part of the lineage itself.

This is you.

You are an astrologer of the highest order. A mythologist. An academic. A master of your craft. Poring over ancient texts that would make most of us weep in exasperation at the cumbersome and sometimes mistranslated works of our astrological ancestors, you have the kind of patience it takes to listen to and decipher the voices of our past for the rest of us.

You are a teacher's teacher.

Studying with you connected me to a history I did not know I was missing. Studying with you connected me to techniques that clarified not only my craft but my own life's purpose. Studying with you helped me to understand the simple, specific, and straightforward messages of my chart. I had stared at the thing for twenty-six years and still felt unsure of its specific directives. Until you, I couldn't really grasp the writing on the wall—or in the sky.

Anything that I have learned to do well as an astrologer can always be traced back to your painstaking efforts in teaching me, and the world, about the profound beauty and wisdom of astrology. I am forever grateful for you, and always thankful for any time spent with you.

APPENDIX I
EACH SIGN AND ITS SYMBOL, MODALITY, ELEMENT, AND PLANETARY RULER

SIGN	MODALITY	ELEMENT	PLANETARY RULER
♈ ARIES	Cardinal	Fire	♂ Mars
♉ TAURUS	Fixed	Earth	♀ Venus
♊ GEMINI	Mutable	Air	☿ Mercury
♋ CANCER	Cardinal	Water	☽ Moon
♌ LEO	Fixed	Fire	☉ Sun
♍ VIRGO	Mutable	Earth	☿ Mercury
♎ LIBRA	Cardinal	Air	♀ Venus
♏ SCORPIO	Fixed	Water	♂ Mars
♐ SAGITTARIUS	Mutable	Fire	♃ Jupiter
♑ CAPRICORN	Cardinal	Earth	♄ Saturn
♒ AQUARIUS	Fixed	Air	♄ Saturn
♓ PISCES	Mutable	Water	♃ Jupiter

PLANET	DOMICILE	DETRIMENT	EXALTATION	FALL
☉ SUN	Leo	Aquarius	Aries	Libra
☽ MOON	Cancer	Capricorn	Taurus	Scorpio
☿ MERCURY	Gemini Virgo	Sagittarius Pisces	Virgo	Pisces
♀ VENUS	Taurus Libra	Aries Scorpio	Pisces	Virgo
♂ MARS	Aries Scorpio	Taurus Libra	Capricorn	Cancer
♃ JUPITER	Sagittarius Pisces	Gemini Virgo	Cancer	Capricorn
♄ SATURN	Capricorn Aquarius	Cancer Leo	Libra	Aries

10th House
Career and public roles

9th House
Travel, education, publishing, religion, astrology, and philosophy

8th House
Death, mental health, and other people's resources

11th House
Community and good fortune

7th House
Committed partnerships

12th House
Sorrows, loss, and hidden life

1st House
Self, appearance, vitality, and life force

6th House
Work and health

2nd House
Assets, resources, and self-worth

5th House
Sex, children, and creative energy

3rd House
Communication, daily rituals, siblings, and extended family

4th House
Parents, home, and foundations

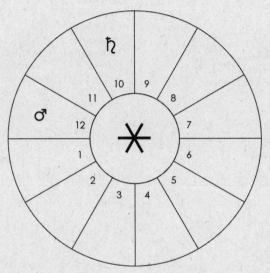

Planets in houses at a 60-degree angle from each other are sextile.

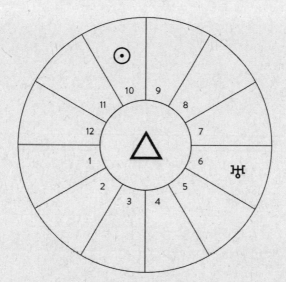

Planets in houses at a 120-degree angle from each other are trine.

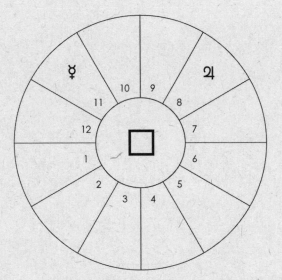

Planets in houses at a 90-degree angle from each other are square.

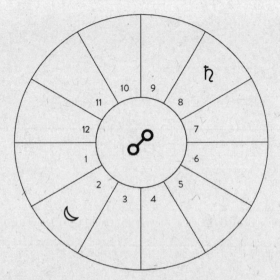

Planets in houses at a 180-degree angle from each other are in opposition.

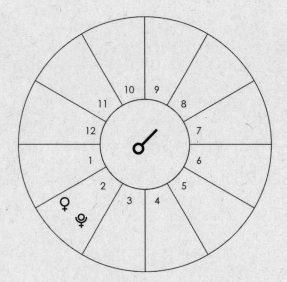

Planets in the same house are conjunct.

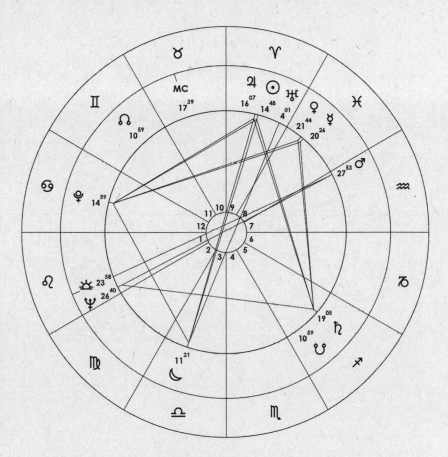

DR. MAYA ANGELOU'S BIRTH CHART

Birth Date and Time: April 4, 1928, at 2:10 p.m.

Location: St. Louis, Missouri, USA

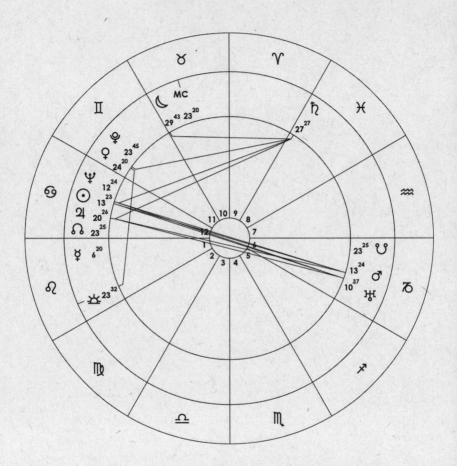

FRIDA KAHLO'S BIRTH CHART

Birth Date and Time: July 6, 1907, at 8:30 a.m.

Location: Coyoacán, Mexico City, Mexico

INDEX

C

Cancer: as cardinal sign, 22; as a water sign, 25; Jupiter as ruler in, 220–21; Mars as ruler in, 216–17; Moon in, 107–9; Moon ruled by, 158; nature of the Moon in its domicile in, and, 26; Jupiter in its exaltation in, 26; relationship of Fall, Mars, and, 26; rising, 167–69, 200–201; Saturn as ruler in, 228–29; sensitive and caring style of, 21; Sun in, 48–50

Capricorn: as a cardinal sign, 22; as an earth sign, 24; enduring and reserved style of, 21; Jupiter as ruler in, 223; Mars as ruler in, 214; Moon in, 117–19; nature of the Moon in its detriment in, 26; relationship of Exaltation, Mars, and, 26; relationship of Fall, Jupiter, and, 26; rising, 179–81; Saturn as ruler in, 60, 61, 159, 226–37; Sun in, 60–62

cardinal signs: Aries, 22; Cancer, 22; Capricorn, 22; Libra, 22

career: Ascendant ruler in the 10th house representing work and, 247–48; author's journey toward finding her, 6–7; Frida Kahlo exalted Moon in 10th house driving, 123, 139–40; Moon in the 10th house on, 135–36; Sun in the 10th house on, 77–78; 10th

house representing public roles and, 27, 28, 29. *See also* work

caregivers. *See* parents/caregivers, the Moon

challenges (squares and oppositions): oppositions from your Moon, 148–50; oppositions from your Sun, 89–91; reflection questions on, 95, 155; squares from your Moon, 145–47; squares from your Sun, 87–89

ChaniNicholas.com: look up your natal chart on, 11. *See also* natal charts

Check In With Your Chart: your Ascendant, 161; your Moon, 100; your Sun, 39

children: Ascendant ruler in the 5th house representing, 239–40; 5th house representing, 27, 29; Moon in the 5th house representing, 128–29; Sun in the 5th house representing, 72–73

committed partnerships: Ascendant ruler in the 7th house representing, 242–44; Moon in the 7th house representing, 131–32; 7th house representing, 27, 29; Sun in the 7th house representing, 74–75

communication: Ascendant ruler in the 3rd house and, 236–37; element of a sign indicates, 23; Mars in Aquarius and courageous, 217;

E

D

representing, 27, 29, 67, 69, 125, 127, 235–36; Sun in Capricorn to utilize your, 60; Sun in Leo to access all its, 50; Sun in Pluto and obsession with accumulating, 94; Sun in Taurus building, 44; Sun in Virgo and 2nd house, 67; Taurus rising and ability to stabilize available, 164. *See also* livelihood

rising sign. *See* Ascendant

S

Sagittarius: adventurous and expansive style of, 21; as a fire sign, 23; Jupiter as ruler in, 159, 219–20; Mercury as ruler in, 203–4; Moon in, 116–17; as a mutable sign, 23; as rising sign, 177–79; Sun in, 58–60

Saturn: Moon conjunction with, 153; opposition from your Moon to, 149–50; opposition from your Sun, 90; relationship of homes, signs, and, 26; a sextile from your Moon to, 141; sextile from your Sun to, 84; signs and styles affecting, 21; square from your Moon to, 147; square from your Sun to, 88; the Taskmaster role of, 20; trine from your Moon to, 144; trine from your Sun to, 86; your Sun conjunction with, 93

Saturn as ruler: Aquarius, 62, 159, 226, 227; Aries, 230; Cancer, 228–29; Capricorn, 60, 61, 159, 226–37; description of, 225–26; Leo, 228, 229–30; Libra, 227–28; in all other signs, 230–31

Scorpio: as a fixed sign, 22; intense and penetrating style of, 21; Mars as ruler in, 159, 212–14; Moon in, 114–15; as a water sign, 25; relationship of Fall, Moon, and, 26; rising, 175–77; Sun in, 56–58; Venus as ruler as, 207–8

2nd house: Ascendant ruler in, 235–36; description of, 27; as house of assets, resources and self-worth, 27, 29, 67, 69, 125, 127, 235–36; Moon in the, 125–26; Sun in the, 69–70; natal chart illustration including the, 29

secrets: Ascendant ruler in the 12th house representing, 250–51; Frida Kahlo's Sun in the 12th house of, 232–33; Sun in the 12th house representing, 79–80; 12th house representing, 28, 29

self: cannot be expressed without planet conjunctions with Sun, 81; developing relationship between money, livelihood, and, 67; finding balance between other and, 54; 1st house representing body, vitality, and, 27, 29, 68–69; learning to connect with physical, 63; Sun is our essential, 40, 60, 68